WITHDRAWN
FROM STOCK

Feminism

Modern Ideologies

FEMINISM

John Charvet
Reader in Political Science,
London School of Economics and Political Science

J.M. Dent & Sons Ltd
London, Melbourne and Toronto

2705

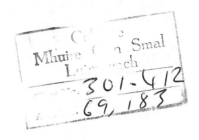

Mhuire   Smal
L   ch
301-412
69,183

First published 1982
© John Charvet, 1982

All rights reserved
Printed in Great Britain by
Biddles Ltd, Guildford, Surrey, for
J.M. Dent & Sons Ltd
Aldine House, 33 Welbeck Street, London W1M 8LX
This book is set in 11/12½ Compugraphic Plantin by
Datamove Ltd, Acton

This book if bound as a paperback is subject to the
condition that it may not be issued on loan or otherwise
except in its original binding

British Library Cataloguing in Publication Data

Charvet, John
  Feminism.
  1. Feminism—History
  I. Title
  305.4'2'09   HQ1154

  ISBN 0-460-10255-9
  ISBN 0-460-11255-4 Pbk

Contents

Contents

Acknowledgments

I am very grateful to Elizabeth Vallance for giving me the benefit of her knowledge and understanding of feminism in commenting upon an earlier version of this work; to my sister, Anne Charvet, and my wife, Barbara Charvet, for their attempts to help me see and write more clearly on this subject; to my editor, Jocelyn Burton, for her sound advice and scrupulous attention; and to my secretary, Paula da Gama Pinto, for her invariably efficient typing and retyping of versions of this work.

Introduction

This book is a study of the main feminist doctrines of the last two hundred years. It is not a study of feminist movements, but of the basic ideas to be found in major feminist works, such as Mary Wollstonecraft's *A Vindication of the Rights of Woman*, J. S. Mill's *The Subjection of Women* and Simone de Beauvoir's *The Second Sex*. These ideas will be studied, not as purely historical entities on which the historian forbears to make critical evaluations, and certainly not as ideologies whose worth is to be understood only in relation to the practical aims of the thinkers and their adherents, but as serious contributions to an understanding of the ethical basis of relations between men and women.

Broadly, the essential idea of feminism is the equality of woman with man.[1] But the idea of equality is far from perspicuous, and a more adequate formulation of the basic idea is that women have equal worth with men in respect of their common nature as free persons. From this fundamental equality of value is derived a claim to an equality of rights or, more vaguely, of position in society, whether the rights or position are conceived in liberal and individualist or in socialist terms.

Two objections might be found to this initial identification of the feminist idea. Firstly, there are anti-feminist writers who deny that women are in any way inferior to men, and who may go so far as to say that they are of equal worth. But they mean by this that men and women have very different natures with different needs, and that their equal claims are to the fulfilment of these natures. Thus are justified the separate and traditional spheres of men and women, by which the public worlds of economic and political society with their appropriate rights are reserved to men, and women are directed to the household and the family. However, in so far as the idea of equality, or the denial of inequality, makes its appearance in this type of argu-

1

ment, it is not the same as that idea of equal worth of men and women in respect of their common nature as free persons specified above. For, in effect, the argument supposes that only men are free and rational beings whose nature requires fulfilment in a public world of action, while women's nature and virtues are emotional and passive. This view justifies the age-old subordination and inferiority of woman, but instead of arguing for it straightforwardly on the grounds of woman's natural inferiority, it pays lip-service to modern egalitarianism, whose basic element is the rejection of such arguments. It is, however, lip-service only.

Secondly, there are those writers who might be considered feminist and who, whether seriously or not, claim for women not a position of equality with men, but one of superiority, and hence the subjection of men to women; or even conceive the fantasy of eliminating men altogether.[2] However, although there is much hostility to men and hatred of them as an oppressive class in the contemporary radical feminist movement, this does not itself involve a commitment to reverse the oppression, or to eliminate the oppressors. The movement is committed rather to the elimination of the oppression in the form of any sexual differentiation of roles in human society. This is only an extreme form of the egalitarian idea, and to be distinguished from the inegalitarian or murderous fantasies of others, which I shall not consider further.[3]

The basic feminist idea, then, as I understand it, is that in respect of their fundamental worth there is no difference between men and women. At this level there are not male beings and female beings, but only human beings or persons. The nature and value of persons is independent of gender. In my initial formulation I called such persons free. The meaning and importance of the free nature of equal persons will, I hope, become clear in the course of the work, but something needs to be said by way of preliminary elucidation. The identification of equal persons as free points to the way in which equal worth is to be understood. For by equality is not meant that human beings have the same mental and physical capacities. Whether or not some are mentally or physically superior to others is irrelevant to the validity of the claim to equal worth. This claim means firstly that as free beings individuals are capable of directing themselves to ends of their own choosing, and secondly that in respect of this capacity for self-direction individuals have the same worth. The question of how this capacity is to be exercised and equal value realized in society produces the major political divisions in the theory and practice of the modern world. A socialist will tend to understand the freedom of self-direction in terms of the collective act of individuals as members of society; whereas those belonging to what I call the individualist tradition conceive it in terms of an individual's choices for his own life within a framework of law which guarantees an equal right to all to make such choices. However, for both the socialist and individualist traditions the freedom and equality of individuals are the fundamental values.

The feminist idea understood in the above terms is undeniably the product of ideas about the nature of man and about the ethical basis of his relations in society, which were developed in the early modern period, in the seventeenth and eighteenth centuries, and which although affirmed of man generically, were in effect taken to apply only to men. The first form which these ideas took, for instance in the natural rights school of John Locke, can be called individualist, in that the ethical basis of social relations is understood to lie in the value that each man has in himself as an independent individual apart from his relations to others in society, and the specific forms of social and political life are derived from the rights that are held to pertain to this independent individuality. Individualist social and political theory, however, very soon came under attack at the beginning of the nineteenth century from the new standpoint of socialism. As I have claimed above, the new socialist ideas did not involve the rejection of the ideas of either freedom or equality. They involved rather the rejection of the idea that these values pertain to individuals as such apart from their existence as social beings, and that they are to be realized by individual rather than by co-operative action.

Individualist and socialist theory in their different forms comprise the two major explanations of the idea of the equal worth of men as free beings. The classic works of nineteenth-

3

century feminist thought are applications of one or other of these theories to the question of the nature of woman and her place in society relative to man. Thus the first two chapters of this book will consider these classic works as different expressions of the individualist interpretation of freedom and equality on the one hand, and of the socialist idea on the other. Feminist thought, as a contribution to ethical philosophy, has to be understood as part of this larger body of thought, and hence an account of this larger body must be given if the idea in feminism is to be intelligible, and if the presuppositions of the different versions are to be criticized.

The third chapter deals with the works of contemporary feminist thought beginning with that of Simone de Beauvoir, but concentrating on the contribution to the debate made by those who call themselves radical feminists.[4] These feminists are inclined to be socialists and might be understood as developing another form of the socialist idea. But this would be to miss their peculiar emphasis which is in some ways quite independent of both individualist and socialist theories. Thus they deny that either of the classic forms of the idea of the liberation of women is in itself sufficient to bring about the desired end. Both these forms, they argue, leave the basic structure of woman's oppression by man largely untouched. This is because they conceive of the liberation of women simply as the extension to women of the forms through which oppressed men achieve their liberation. This, they claim, fails to grasp that the basic cause of women's oppression is not a form of life which oppresses some men also, viz. a lack of civil or political rights, or private property and exploitation of labour, but is a special form of life which the radical feminists call patriarchy, through which men appropriate all superior social roles and keep women in subordinate and exploited positions. Feminism on this view is not the application to the man/woman relation of a more general social theory, but a study of the socio-political formation of patriarchy itself, and will thus constitute a social theory of its own. However, even though on this view the liberation of women requires a class war to be waged against their male oppressors in patriarchy, its attainment, by the overthrow of all sexual differentiation of roles and the advent of an androgynous future, remains an expression of the basic feminist idea of the equal value of men and women as free beings.*

---

* The reader will have noticed that I intend to use the masculine pronoun to do service for individuality in general, both male and female. I have given this matter some thought, and considered, but rejected, the use of the archaism 'one'. The dual he/she, his/her I find clumsy and unattractive. The obvious alternative is to treat the individual as feminine. It seems to me entirely appropriate that women should use the feminine pronoun and men the masculine, and I have acted accordingly.

1 Individualist Feminism

Introduction

Individualist social and political theory developed in the course of the seventeenth century and received one of its most notable and influential expressions in John Locke's *Second Treatise of Government* (1689). Since it was in this form, as modified by Locke's radical and dissenting heirs in eighteenth-century England, that individualist theory was applied to the woman question by Mary Wollstonecraft in the first classic work of feminist thought, it is appropriate to ignore the alternative expressions of individualism and concentrate initially on Locke's thought. Other forms of individualist thought will be touched upon subsequently, but it should be noted now that by concentrating on Locke's thought I do not mean to imply that he is either the sole creator or the typical representative of that theory.

It is also true that Mary Wollstonecraft was not the first to apply the ideas of individualism to the position of women in society. We find a number of women and men in the seventeenth and eighteenth centuries claiming equality for women on the basis of the new ideas.[1] However, as I have indicated, this book is not intended to be a full historical account of feminist thought, but rather an identification of the main doctrines to be found in the major works. Wollstonecraft's *Vindication* is the first substantial treatise in the field.

By individualism I mean the view that understands the basis of social and political order to lie in the possession by individuals of rights. Individuals possess these rights independently of their social relations. Exactly how these rights are acquired is a matter on which different theorists produce conflicting views, and exactly how these rights are to be elaborated in specific social and political forms is also a question which is subject to much disagreement. But the primary content of the rights is generally understood to consist in the freedom of individuals to do what they wish without being interfered with by others. Each individual is reponsible for his own life and must choose it for himself within limits set by the equal rights of others, and within the necessities of a framework of laws and institutions without which such rights would be vain or insecure. It is obvious enough that since one individual's freedom is limited by that of every other, difficulties arise for this theory at a fundamental level. Firstly, there is the problem of how the acceptance by the individual of limitations on his freedom can be made intelligible without undermining the individualist nature of the theory by introducing collectivist elements such as are to be found in the theories of Hobbes and Rousseau. To accept the rights of others as a restraint on his actions the individual must identify his interest with theirs and so acknowledge a common interest to which his own becomes subordinate. Secondly, limitations on individual freedom have to be equal to be just, and the problem arises as to how such equality is to be secured without at the same time becoming opposed to the requirements of freedom. The basic idea affirms the unity of the values of equality and freedom, but elaboration of the idea very quickly brings these into opposition to each other.

These difficulties are to be found everywhere in the history of individualist theory, and will be touched upon further in the course of this work. For the moment, in elucidating Locke's thought, they will be ignored. In Locke's view the basic right to freedom is a natural right residing in the individual as such independently of his membership of any political society. It is a right that individuals possess in the so-called state of nature, which is defined as a state in which no political society or obligation exists. It is not a state of war or savagery, but is rather a natural society governed by a natural law which affirms the right of each man to do what he wants with his life, liberty and possessions without being interfered with by others, so long as he acts within the restraints imposed by the law of equal rights.[2]

The law of nature is God's law and men have rights because God bestows such rights on them. He commands men to seek their own preservation and that of others. But God does not tell them what to do to preserve themselves. Each is to decide for himself, and each has a duty to God not to injure or invade another. Thus although the primary moral relation in Locke's theory consists in the individual's relation to God, men face each other as possessors of rights to non-interference with their freedom. The law of nature is also a law of reason, and is accessible to every man by virtue of his rational being. Every man on attaining maturity is capable of governing himself by his own rational apprehension of the law of nature, and so of becoming an independent and autonomous individual in a natural society of such individuals.

Although every man is capable of self-direction in accordance with rational law, natural society is not in fact as peaceful and harmonious as this conception may at first suggest to us. If it were, political society would be neither necessary nor justifiable. Men, it turns out, are no great observers of the law of nature, and need to create political society to remedy the main deficiencies of the state of nature. These are: the lack of a legislature to specify in a system of detailed law the requirements of the law of nature, of an impartial judiciary and of an effective law-enforcement agency. To achieve these ends men are willing through their own consent to enter into political society and accept its obligations.[3]

Before outlining Locke's conception of political society, something must be said about the rights to property and contract, for these rights give more specific form to the rights individuals have as members of natural society, and determine the civil rights they ought to have in political society. Unless individuals in natural society have a right to the private appropriation and control of the means of satisfying their wants and of realizing their aims, their right to freedom is nugatory. According to Locke then, although God gave the earth and its resources in the first place to mankind as a whole, he cannot have intended to deny individuals the right to appropriate parts of the earth in order to preserve themselves without obtaining the general consent of mankind. Otherwise men would starve to death in the midst of plenty. We must, therefore, presume a right of private appropriation in natural society. In the first instance this right is limited to what an individual can acquire of unappropriated nature through the work of his hands and the labour of his body, subject to the very important provision that he leave enough and as good of the object appropriated for others to satisfy their needs, and provided also that he does not leave anything that he has appropriated to rot away unused.[4]

Locke proceeds to remove these restrictions by an argument concerning the introduction of money in natural society. Money has a value only as a result of the consent of those among whom it is introduced. But its introduction has certain consequences. It enables people to accumulate wealth without allowing any of it to rot. It permits the development of great inequalities of wealth. Since men have consented to the introduction of money, they have thereby consented to its consequences and hence to unequal accumulation.

These arguments should not detain us. My purpose in setting them out here is simply to indicate the way in which, on Locke's view, the basic natural rights of individuals to life, liberty and possessions are to be elaborated in more concrete economic and social practices. Locke justifies a market society in which individuals may accumulate wealth subject to a general requirement on the political authority to have regard to the common good and the welfare of members of society. Whatever an individual has legitimately appropriated he may alienate to another through contract or gift. This freedom of contract applies also to an individual's labour, the products of which become the property of the labourer's master in exchange for wages. Thus the individual is entitled to certain rights to the freedom of his person from injury or from interference to private property and contract. The freedom of the individual both in natural and civil society consists in an order in which those rights prevail.

Political society rests on the consent of its members, firstly to join together in an association founded on a common will, and secondly to the formation of specific constitutional powers comprising an elected legislature and a separate executive. It appears, although none too clearly, that only property owners are to be accounted full members of political society with political rights in respect of the election and responsibility of the supreme legislative power. All men should have equal civil rights, yet in the political sphere rights are restricted. Political society exists to give better protection to men's natural rights to life, liberty and possessions. It does not have ends of its own in relation to which men's natural rights may be limited. On the contrary its duty is to transform these general natural rights into a detailed system of civil rights protected by known and impartial judges and efficiently enforced.

There can be no doubt that for Locke it is men only who are to enjoy the full range of civil and political rights. Yet he nowhere argues that women are less qualified than men for the possession of those natural rights, which are the ground for the enjoyment of civil and political rights. Women enter the argument only at the point at which he discusses the family. Here he takes particular trouble to insist that the child is subject to the joint parental authority of husband and wife, and not to the authority of a single patriarch.[5] Indeed, marriage is presented as a contract between independent persons.[6] This implies that the woman has the same basic rights of independent personality as the man, that is to say the right to do what she likes with her life within the constraints of the law of nature. For if marriage is a contract, the union which it constitutes rests solely on the consent of the parties to it, just as the union of political society does. These parties must in the first instance be free and equal self-governing persons in relation to the union. Otherwise their consent could not create the union.

The reason why Locke is inclined to a liberal view of marriage, while in no other way accepting the equal claims of women with men, is, it is reasonable to suppose, because of the correspondence between political society and the family. His individualist arguments in respect of civil and political society are directed in part against a patriarchal conception of political authority as expressed in the work of Sir Robert Filmer. The *First Treatise of Government* is a refutation of Filmer's book *Patriarcha*. One of the elements in patriarchal theory is the mutual reinforcement provided by the conception of the king's absolute authority as that of a father ruling his family and by the conception of the father's absolute rule in the family as that of a king over his people. The absolutism of the one is supported by the absolutism of the other. Since Locke's aim is the replacement of absolutist ideas by individualist ones, it would not be coherent for him to retain the absolute authority of the father in a family, while abolishing absolute authority in the state: or rather he could do this if he were prepared to argue forthrightly that women were not fully human beings at all and had no rational apprehension of the law of nature. He does not do this.

It should not be supposed, however, that because Locke conceives of marriage as a contract, which implies a certain equality between free persons, equality, for him, pervades the relations between husband and wife within the marriage. A place for the superior position of men is retained. Because the man is the stronger and abler member, he becomes the leader in the partnership.[7] This might be called the constitutional rule of the husband within the family as distinguished from the absolute rule of the patriarch.

The Lockeian conception of marriage contributed to bringing about, in the late seventeenth and the eighteenth century in England, an improvement in the position of women in the family and in society. The contractual view was accepted, but still combined with a traditional subordination of wives to their husbands by the treatment of the contract as one in which the wife promised to be submissive, subject and obedient, in exchange for the husband's undertaking of affection, fidelity and care.[8] Although this no doubt reflects a contract between persons of unequal power or capacities, it does involve a conception of marriage, which Lawrence Stone calls the companionate marriage, based on the mutual affection and care of husband and wife, in which a greater equality than had before existed characterized the relation between the married couple. The companionate marriage was an element in the development of what is popularly known as the nuclear family. Stone calls this the Closed Domesticated Nuclear Family: closed because the boundaries between the immediate nuclear family and the wider kin group and larger society became more marked, and less open to casual and frequent crossing, thus creating the privacy of family life. It is domesticated because more of the life of the family's members was passed in the family home with the other members. Stone further describes the Closed Domesticated Family thus:

> It was a family organized around the principle of personal autonomy, and bound together by strong affective ties. Husbands and wives personally selected each other rather than obeying parental wishes, and their prime motives were now long-term personal

11

affection rather than economic or status advantage for the lineage as a whole. More and more time, energy, money and love of both parents were devoted to the upbringing of children. . . Patriarchal attitudes within the home markedly declined, and greater autonomy was granted not only to children but also to wives.[9]

Stone connects these changes in the nature of family life with what he calls individualism, which he defines as 'a growing introspection and interest in the individual personality; and secondly, a demand for personal autonomy and a corresponding respect for the individual's right to privacy, to self-expression, and to the free exercise of his will within the limits set by the need for social cohesion'.[10] Finally, he suggests that in the companionate marriage of the eighteenth century the conventional ideal of wifely status becomes that of equality.[11]

Yet how far these changes in the conception and practice of marriage were from any radical rethinking of the relations between men and women by the extension to women of the fundamental rights of free persons, which were being claimed increasingly for all men, can be seen in the thought on this matter of that radical individualist and propagandist for the companionate marriage – Jean Jacques Rousseau.

As suggested earlier, Rousseau's individualism is a more complicated affair than Locke's. He does not accept that men have rights in a state of nature prior to the existence of political society, but holds that they acquire rights only in political society. Yet this simply means that the condition of a legitimate political society is the recognition by individual contractants of each other as possessors of rights. Each recognizes the other as a value in himself, and consequently the possessor of the political right to participate as an equal in the legislative decisions of the community, and of the civil right to do what he likes within the limits of the general legislation without interference by others. Rousseau affirms the basic individualist doctrine that each man's 'first law is to watch over his own preservation; his first care he owes to himself, and as soon as he reaches the age of reason, he becomes the only judge of the best means to preserve himself; he becomes his own master'.[12] Thus no man has a natural authority over his fellows, and 'since force alone bestows no right, all legitimate authority among men must be based on covenants'.[13]

Rousseau is famous for his emphasis on equality, and his hatred of all forms of dependence of men on other men through inequality of power or wealth. But equality was necessary for him for the sake of freedom or self-determination. Inequality meant dependence on another, and dependence meant being determined by others rather than by oneself, and hence a loss of freedom. Thus he is opposed to the inequalities of wealth and power that Locke justifies. He thought that only in a small community of homogeneous and economically independent producers could individuals combine to produce a general will which realized the individualist ideal of truly equal rights. In so far as men are subject to such a general will, Rousseau held, they are subject to nothing but the conditions of their own freedom. Hence in willing it, they are free.[14]

Rousseau carried none of this theory of freedom and equality over into an account of the relations between men and women, and he failed to do so not because he avoided the subject, but quite deliberately and explicitly. In his work on education he held that women are not to be brought up to be free persons requiring equality and independence in their relations. They are to be brought up to be dependent on men. Men exist for themselves and are values as such; but women have value only in relation to men. Their education, therefore, must be predominantly concerned with learning how to please men.[15] However, the inferiority of value that Rousseau accords to women is not accompanied by a return to the belief in a patriarchal conception of the family in which the father is an absolute monarch over his wife and children. Rousseau is a powerful advocate of the companionate marriage, and the education he recommends for women is of exactly the same type as the one which the propagandists of the companionate marriage developed as a way of producing wives who would be fitting companions for their husbands. Women should have sufficiently cultivated minds to be able to enter into agreeable and intelligent conversation with their husbands, without which the husband will cease to find any pleasure in being at home. At the same time the wife should not be so well educated as to have a mind and opinions of her own, and so become 'une fille savante et bel-esprit'.[16] Her education will involve a superficial cultivation, primarily of the arts, so as to give her an acquaintance with culture, but no independent command of it. This was precisely the sort of education for girls that developed in the eighteenth century together with the progress of the companionate marriage. Just as in Rousseau's thought, so more generally, the primary argument of its advocates was that it would make women better and more agreeable wives for their husbands, and also more intelligent mothers for their children.[17]

Rousseau's arguments for women as of purely relative value are based on the conception of her as primarily a sexual and not a human being. In everything that does not concern sex, he says, men and women are identical, but in respect of her sexual nature woman is made to please man. Woman is made to arouse sexual desire in the man, and not conversely. She has the natural sexual instinct to please the man, whereas it is man's nature to attain his object by superior force. At the same time woman is by nature more chaste than man, and is governed by shame, the function of which is to control the violence of the male passion once it is aroused.

The importance of these observations lies in the claim that the male is a sexual being only at certain times in his life, and he is otherwise a free being or person, while the female is female throughout her child-bearing life. It is this fact that ensures the dominance in her of her sexual nature, because of which she cannot be a value in herself, but only a value relative to a man.

It is evident, however, that Rousseau implicitly admits the injustice of this state of affairs. For if woman is in everything that does not pertain to her sexual nature identical to man, she must be potentially more than a sexual being, and have the same capacity and need for freedom as man. That she is dominated by her sexual function within the family is not essential to her nature as a human being, but a consequence of at most only part of her nature. Rousseau is frequently criticized for not applying his ideas of freedom and equality to the relation between men and women, and for so grossly denying the free personality of woman.[18] Such criticisms are certainly valid. However, by implication he admits that woman has the potentiality for freedom. The implicit logic of Rousseau's position is that this freedom is incompatible with woman's life and function in the family. Since he does not consider the possibility of any alteration in the latter, it follows that woman cannot be educated for freedom and must be educated for dependence.

Mary Wollstonecraft (1759–1797)

Mary Wollstonecraft was born in London, where as a young woman trying to support herself by running a school, she came under the influence of a circle of radical Dissenters whose leading figure was Dr Price.[19] These thinkers may be called the radical heirs of the Lockeian natural rights school. They used Lockeian arguments to demand full equality of civil and political rights for men, and the abolition of all aristocratic privileges which interfered with the operation of equality of opportunity in the sense of careers open to talents. They were middle-class democrats with an individualist social and political theory. They welcomed enthusiastically the American, and in its early stages the French Revolution. This enthusiasm Wollstonecraft shared. Her first publication had been a work on the education of women (1786), but with the outbreak of the French Revolution she quickly joined in the crowd of those attempting to refute the arguments of Burke's *Reflections on the Revolution in France*, and before affirming the rights of woman published *A Vindication of the Rights of Man* (1790). *A Vindication of the Rights of Woman* followed closely (1792).

The basic idea in the latter work is the affirmation that women are first and foremost *human* beings and not sexual beings. Given that this is a statement made within an individualist conception of what a human being is, the main lines of her argument follow from this premise. Thus woman's primary end must be fulfilment as a human being and not as a woman. In this respect women are exactly like men, whose primary end no one claims to be male but only to be human.[20]

The basis for Wollstonecraft's claim that women are human beings is that they are rational creatures. They are capable of governing themselves by reason. Man's superiority to the brutes consists in his reason, and it is in respect of his rational capacities that natural rights are claimed for men. Hence if women are to be denied natural rights, it must be proved that they have no rational capacity.[21] It is not sufficient to say that women's particular talents

15

are in general inferior to those of men, for it does not follow from such inferiority that they are not rational beings, capable of governing themselves, and hence that they do not have the rights of rational beings, any more than it follows that the inferiority of talent of some men to others is a ground for denying their nature and rights as human beings. Wollstonecraft does not, of course, accept the view that women in general do have inferior talents to men. If in the present state of society it appears that they are less talented, this is hardly surprising given the age-old neglect from which women have suffered. Women's real capacities can be determined only when they have been given their freedom, and the opportunity and education to develop their talents.[22]

One of the main elements in the view of those, who, like Rousseau, wish to deny the primacy of the common nature of men and women, is the claim that the virtues of men and women are not the same. While the virtues of a man are primarily those of a rational being, the virtues of a woman, it is argued, are those relative to her primarily sexual nature – namely chastity, gentleness, and obedience. But, as Wollstonecraft argues, if we now see a woman as primarily rational and human, we must accept that her virtues and duties are fundamentally the same as a man's. Human virtue is one and the same for both men and women. It is reason which teaches us what this virtue is, and hence no human being can be virtuous in whom this rationality has not been developed. Such rational conduct is the perfection of human nature, and the condition of human happiness.

To govern oneself by reason, Wollstonecraft says, is to achieve independence, 'the grand blessing of life, the basis of every virtue',[23] because thereby one is depedent only on one's own reason and not on the opinions and judgments of others. To obtain this grand blessing the education of a person's rational powers is essential. The most perfect education is one which enables individuals to achieve this independence. As she notes, this is Rousseau's view of the desirable life for men, and what she is doing, she says, is extending this conception to women.[24] However, Wollstonecraft's problem and that of nineteenth-century individualist feminism in general is to give a plausible account of why this independence does not require a life for woman in civil and political society which is identical to man's, and so of how independence for women is compatible with the continued existence of the family and of woman's traditional roles within it.

Wollstonecraft spends most of the work elucidating the ways in which society's existing conception of the appropriate education and way of life for women conspires to prevent the development in women of their human capacities and virtues – a theme which becomes a standard element, variously elaborated, in subsequent feminist thought of every persuasion. For if woman is essentially a free rational being like a man, and yet existing women are not actually like this, then it is because society moulds them in accordance with a false conception of their nature. In relation to woman's true nature and potential the result is a corruption and a degradation. For Wollstonecraft, because woman is seen by existing society primarily as a sexual and not as a human being, she is educated to acquire qualities that fit her for a relation of dependence on man. She is brought up to learn how to please man, to charm him by her grace and beauty, and her virtues are those of gentleness, docility and a spaniel-like affection. Woman, as she actually is, is a weak, dependent and emotional creature, but as she is, she is an artificial product of these male ideas and arrangements. Wollstonecraft acknowledges the great power of education and environment in the determination of character. But she does not assert that human beings have no nature and are simply whatever they are made by their environment. For, as we have seen, she holds that they are inherently free rational beings. However, this is a potential which has to be actualized.

Women are brought up to be physically feeble, Wollstonecraft continues her indictment, not to take exercise, to be attentive only to their physical appearance. They are taught from their infancy that a woman's value lies in her beauty, and that it is through the power of her charms that she must subject men. Their minds are shaped by this concern, and as a result become as feeble and dependent as their bodies. Their education neglects their understanding and inflames their senses. Hence they develop over-exercised sensibilities and are subject to the emotions and feelings of the moment, quite unable to control themselves by reason or judgment.

One aspect of woman's education that in Wollstonecraft's view does more mischief than all the rest is the lack of order in it. To do everything in an orderly manner is a most important precept, but women rarely succeed in following it to the same extent as men, who, Wollstonecraft thinks, are broken into method from infancy. By not acquiring a desire for order women fail to learn to generalize their thoughts, and hence to develop their understanding. The folly and emotionalism of women is the result of this narrowness of mind. It is further exacerbated by their way of life. They are confined in the cage of home, and do not have pursuits and employments, as men have, which encourage the mind to open and develop. Human character is formed by the nature of the activity that the individual pursues. Thus the rich and women are generally insipid. For a rational creature can be ennobled only by what he has obtained by his own exertions, and just as the rich are born with the privileges of wealth and desire only to be admired for its possession and display, so women are born with sexual privileges and desire only to be observed and admired as sexual objects. To attain a rational human character, however, the exercise of ability and virtue in useful employment is necessary. It is in the middle rank of persons, Wollstonecraft thinks, that this can primarily be found.[25]

Women are not simply held back by their confined life; they are corrupted by it. They combine the servile vices of the dependent classes with the arbitrariness and irrationality of tyrants in the sexual empire they exercise over men. It is an absurd way, she concludes, to produce chaste wives and sensible mothers. As regards chastity, wives, who are taught to please men and yet are soon disregarded by their husbands, will look elsewhere for their admirers. And as to the upbringing of their children, they have evidently no rational plan on which to conduct it.

The fundamental requirement for reform both in society generally, and in respect of woman's position therein, is equality. Equality here means the absence of dependence of one person on another either through the existence of privileged ranks, which legally subject some to others, or through extremes of wealth and poverty, which turns a formal equality of rights into a sham. The equality needed in society is nevertheless in the first place a formal equality of civil rights, an equality of opportunity for persons to develop their talents and exercise them in any profession or activity they please. Secondly, in desiring the avoidance of extremes of material inequality Wollstonecraft follows Rousseau rather than Locke. Yet in her general conception of the individual's activity in civil rather than political society, that is to say in the primarily economic sphere, she does not adopt Rousseau's hostility to commercial life and the interdependence of individuals in market society, but rather endorses the spirit and enterprise of the middle classes. She acknowledges frankly that her philosophy is particularly appropriate to the middle classes, but that is because, in her view, they are in the best position for achieving rational independence and virtue.

Women are to participate in the enjoyment of equal civil rights. In respect of political rights, however, Wollstonecraft says nothing very much or very clearly. She thinks that 'women ought to have representatives, instead of being arbitrarily governed without having any direct share allowed them in the deliberations of government'.[26] But she does not explain what form of representation she has in mind and whether this would involve a straightforward equality of political rights with men. Her unfulfilled intention was to pursue this question in a later work. Considering, then, formal equality of civil rights only, the problem is how the effective enjoyment of equal rights is to be made compatible with marriage and the family. How are equality and independence to be achieved in the marriage relation itself?

Wollstonecraft says that women must in some degree be independent of their husbands or they will never be virtuous persons or even good wives and mothers. But what does this independence 'in some degree' amount to? In the first place, the education of women will have been reformed so as to give to girls the same discipline as is given to their brothers, and indeed in the same schools and by the same teachers. Their education will thus fit them, as it fits their brothers, for the exercise of some profession, such as those of medicine and midwifery, or for engagement in trade, business or farming. Yet for the most part women, Wollstonecraft accepts, will be called upon to fulfil the duties of wife and mother, and it will be women of superior quality only who will have the road open to pursue extensive plans of usefulness and independence. For most women the values of equality and independence must be realized in the fulfilment of their duties in the family. How does Wollstonecraft envisage this?

Firstly, the wife will no longer be in law the total dependent of her husband, but will be recognized as an equal and responsible person in the marriage in respect of property rights. Secondly, having the capacity to look after herself by earning her own living a woman will not have entered marriage as the only means of subsistence available to her. A woman's independent earning power, even if not made active during the marriage, ensures that she is not totally dependent on her husband's bounty for subsistence either in his life or after his death. Thirdly, in the rational exercise of her traditional functions of wife and mother, managing the household and rearing children, she has a sufficient scope for the realization of her human nature and virtue. Each partner of the marriage will be equally necessary and independent because each fulfils the respective duties of his or her station, he as supporter of the family through his employment, she as wife and mother. Wollstonecraft calls up in her imagination the picture of an ideal family in a better world in which the mother nurses her own children and discharges the duties of her station with perhaps only a servant maid to take off her hands the servile part of the household business. The husband returns home in the evening weary from productive work to smiling babies and a clean hearth.[27]

In desiring for women a life in which they can exercise their reason, Wollstonecraft has no intention of taking them out of their families. The rearing of children, she says, has justly been insisted on as the peculiar destination of women.[28] But with their present education and way of life, such a career is precisely what they are inadequately prepared for. Their ignorance, excessive sensibility, and lack of developed reason unfits them for the task. They need a grasp of the moral duties of life, together with a rational plan for the development of the child. Wollstonecraft's new woman with an educated mind, independent character and capacity for self-support will marry for affection and with respect for her husband and, instead of being idolized as a pure angel while being despised as an inferior mind, will be a better companion to her husband and mother to her children.[29]

We see, then, that Wollstonecraft's radical stance expressed in the demand for equality and independence leads to a conception of a woman's life which turns out to be for the most part an extension of the idea of the companionate marriage and the closed domesticated nuclear family. Her argument for women's rights and education can be seen as an account of those changes that are necessary in order the better to realize that conception of marriage and the family in which the solicitous care of the children's development and the lasting affection of husband and wife are the central binding elements. To achieve the companionate marriage woman needs to be recognized not as an equal in respect of the marriage alone, but as an equal in her own right as a free and rational being, and this itself requires a different education and a different position for her in society generally. In order to be a free and equal person, she must have the rights of a person, and this means equal civil, and probably political, rights with men. But, of course, it makes no sense to say that the point of affirming the rights and destiny of woman as a human being is in order that she may simply fulfil the functions of wife and mother, and hence continue to exist solely as a relative being. The relationship, as Wollstonecraft recognizes, has to be seen the other way round. Woman's primary 'task' is that of a human being to realize her potential for rational and virtuous conduct. However, her destiny as a human being can be fulfilled, although it need not be fulfilled, in her functions as wife and mother.

The Declaration of the Rights of Woman

In the course of the nineteenth century in Europe and America more and more women organized themselves into political movements with the object of obtaining changes in their country's laws which would accord to women the basic civil and political rights demanded by the doctrine of individualist feminism.[30] Many expressions of the individualist belief in the equality of women grounded in their nature as free rational beings were published.[31] A notable public pronouncement of their case was the Declaration of Sentiments formulated by the Women's Rights Convention held at Seneca Falls in America in 1848. It follows the opening of the United States Declaration of Rights with a

21

significant addition:

> We hold these truths to be self-evident: that all men and women are created equal; that they are endowed by their Creator with certain inalienable rights; that among these are life, liberty and the pursuit of happiness: that to secure these rights governments are instituted, deriving their just powers from the consent of the governed...

The declaration proceeds to an enumeration of those rights of which women have been deprived.

> The history of mankind is a history of repeated injuries and usurpations on the part of man toward woman, having in direct object the establishment of an absolute tyranny over her. To prove this, let facts be submitted to a candid world. He has never permitted her to exercise her inalienable right to the elective franchise.
>
> He has compelled her to submit to laws in the formation of which she had no voice...
>
> He has made her, if married, in the eye of the law, civilly dead.
>
> He has taken from her all right in property, even to the wages she earns.
>
> He has made her, morally, an irresponsible being, as she can commit many crimes with impunity, provided they be done in the presence of her husband.
>
> In the covenant of marriage she is compelled to promise obedience to her husband, he becoming to all intents and purposes, her master.
>
> He has so formed the laws of divorce as to what shall be the proper causes, and in case of separation, to whom the guardianship of the children shall be given, as to be wholly regardless of the happiness of women...
>
> He has monopolized all the profitable employments, and from those she is permitted to follow, she receives but a scanty remuneration. He closes against her all the avenues to wealth and distinction which he considers most honourable to himself.
>
> He has denied her the facilities for obtaining a thorough education, all colleges being closed against her.
>
> He allows her in church, as well as state, but a subordinate position...
>
> He has created a false public sentiment by giving to the world a different code of morals for men and women...
>
> He has endeavoured, in every way that he could, to destroy her confidence in her own powers, to lessen her self-respect, and to make her willing to lead a dependent and abject life.[32]

The Declaration proceeds to demand the rectification of these injustices and the restoration to women of their full rights as citizens of the United States. Here then, is an expression of individualist feminist beliefs whose roots are to be found in the Lockeian conception of natural rights. Men and women possess equal basic rights to life, liberty and the pursuit of happiness. God bestowed such rights upon them by enjoining each person to be responsible for his own life and not to interfere in the exercise by others of their rights. From these basic rights are derived more particular rights, to property, freedom of occupation, political representation and so on. However, the belief in the same range of individual rights can be supported in other ways than by an appeal to God-given inalienable natural rights. In the early American feminist, Margaret Fuller, we find a more complex justifying ground for individualist demands.

Margaret Fuller (1810–1850)

Margaret Fuller was born and brought up in New England and received under the direction of her father an intellectual education which enabled her to participate in the formation of the Transcendentalist circle in Boston in the 1840s. She became the editor of their review called *The Dial*, and wrote for this journal in 1843 an essay on women, which she subsequently enlarged and published in 1845 in book form as *Woman in the Nineteenth Century*.

Transcendentalism in America derived from the philosophy of Kant and that of the post-Kantian German Idealists. Kant himself is to be classed as an individualist, albeit of a much more metaphysical nature than either Locke or Rousseau. But the German Idealists, beginning with Fichte and ending with Hegel, developed doctrines of a cosmic mind, of which finite human beings are particular manifestations, which involved an abandonment of individualism. In such doctrines the emergence of a socialist conception of the relation of the individual to the whole can be identified. Thus it might be considered more appropriate to include a discussion of Fuller in a transitional position between individualist and socialist feminism. However, the emphasis in Fuller's feminism falls very much on the ideal of individual freedom and self-development, and on the individual rights considered to be necessary for the realization of this freedom. The conception of the unifying One, and of the individual human being's relation to it, is left very vague, and given no institutional form. It is true that Fuller was interested in early socialist doctrine, as it was to be found in the ideas of Fourier,[33] and in the attempt of a group of transcendentalists to realize these ideas in the Brook Farm experiment near Boston. But she specifically withheld approval of the experiment's fundamental principles.[34] Thus it is more sensible to treat Fuller as an individualist, albeit one whose thought is already pushing beyond the limits of individualism.

The transcendentalists in America were radical reformers, pro-abolitionists and feminists.[35] Fuller, however, in respect of these feminist beliefs, was not so much drawing on the views of others as formulating the transcendentalist position on the subject herself. Nevertheless it is true that her basic conception of the individuality and needs of woman is simply the transcendentalist conception of individuality in respect of man taken over and applied to woman.

The fundamental need of woman, Fuller says, is for freedom. Her need as a woman is not to have power, but for her nature to grow, for her intellect to develop, and for her soul to live free and unimpeded. The aim is self-dependence to be attained through self-help and self-respect. The freedom is the freedom of the universe, to use its means, to learn its secret with God alone for guide and judge, and thus to be dependent on no other human being. Woman, like man, is an infinite being, an end in herself and therefore must not be treated with an exclusive view to any one relation, but always in relation to herself as an end. If her powers as such a free being are developed, she will be fit for any and every relation to which she may be called. As an infinite being she is not made just for one relation or for several, but transcends all such specific relations.

Fuller is expressing here notions of the meaning and value of individuality, which, while implicit in the Lockeian position, are fully developed only by Kant. For Locke the individual has a right to do what he likes with his life without asking leave or depending upon the will of any other individual. Others may not interfere in the exercise of his right to do what he wants. At the same time the individual's freedom depends on his recognition of the equal freedom of others, so that he must restrict his wants within the limits imposed by such an equality of right. This commits the individual to giving priority to the law of equality over his own interest, whenever his wants conflict with the rights of others. Such conflict is bound to occur. What an individual wants for himself may on some occasions be compatible with what others want for themselves; but there can be no guarantee of such harmony. But if the condition of the individual's right is that he subordinate his interest to the law which demands respect for the interest of others, the question arises as to how such self-limitation is possible, and how it is compatible with the individual's freedom. Locke says that it is because the law is a law of reason, and because the individual is a rational being, that one can govern oneself in accordance with it. But since Locke says nothing further in elaboration of this answer, it is clear that he fails to grasp the radical distinction and opposition, which is implicit in this individualist conception of the right to freedom, between the individual's nature and right as a particular being concerned with his own interest, and his nature and right as a moral being concerned with the equal rights of all. Locke appears to think that there is a natural harmony between the individual's particular and moral nature, and that any conflict is the product of particular and contingent circumstances which can be remedied. For Kant, however, this opposition within the individual is the central element in his thought.

The opposition consists in the fact that as a moral being the individual must pursue the equal value of all individuals, while as this particular being he is concerned only with his own wants, whatever they may be. The right of the individual is both to do what he wants without regard to others, and to value others' wants equally with his own. But the wants of individuals are inherently liable to conflict, and thus each individual will necessarily be limited and restricted by the others. Since the basic right of each resides in the individual taken as a single and independent unit, it is established without reference to any such limitation by others, and cannot recognize it. Yet as a moral

69,18

being the individual follows the law of equality and restricts his wants accordingly. Thus as a particular being the individual does not recognize what as a moral being defines his nature.

Morality involves the constraint of one's particular desires by the law of equality, but the possibility of morality appears problematic when the particular and moral natures of the individual are seen as so radically opposed. It is for this reason that Kant rejects any attempt to explain how morality is possible in terms of enlightened self-interest or feelings of benevolence. Such views appeal to the particular nature of individuals which may or may not cohere with the demands of the moral law. To make the moral law dependent upon the possession by the individual of certain contingent desires or feelings would be to destroy its character as unconditionally legislative for the particular will. Moral action for Kant must consist in doing one's duty for its own sake alone. This is the good will which has no other motive than to realize the good.

But how is the good will possible? There must be, Kant says, a pure practical reason, a rational principle which is capable of determining the will to action independently of anything else. This is the categorical imperative. All practical principles for Kant are imperatives: they command a course of action. Empirical practical principles command only conditionally because they depend on the acceptance by the individual of the end to be brought about by following the principle. A categorical imperative commands unconditionally because it is independent of any end apart from its own nature as rational law. It must command simply in respect of its form as law. The categorical imperative says: 'Act only that maxim whereby thou canst at the same time will that it should become a universal law.'[36] Since the maxim must command unconditionally, it must command without qualification and hence universally.

This shows what must be the case if the good will is to be possible. It still does not explain how the individual can be determined to action by respect for the pure idea of law. Clearly if it is the individual as an empirical self-interested being who is to be determined to action, there is no answer. For the pure moral motive to exist, the individual must be not only such a self-interested being, but also a pure rational self with ends entirely different from those which he has as a particular empirical being. Thus, Kant says, if the categorical imperative is to be possible, we need the notion of an end of action that is unconditional because it is an end of absolute worth. Kant affirms the existence of such an end: 'Man and generally any rational being exists as an end in himself, not merely as a means to be arbitrarily used by this or that will.'[37] Man is an end of absolute worth, because he is a pure rational being, so that the foundation of the pure practical principle is that 'rational nature exists as an end in itself'.[38]

Moral action for Kant consists in the striving of rational nature in men to give itself existence and hence to realize its infinite worth. This is the free, self-determining individual. In some of the post-Kantians the nature of this self as pure reason is obscured, and a more intuitive and mystical interpretation of the inner infinite being of the individual is presented. Furthermore, in the case of the Idealists beginning with Fichte the inner being is understood, not as an individual's immortal soul, but as a universal mind which underlies and is the ground of all particular individuals, whose striving to achieve absolute value is conceived of as the attempt to realize this universal mind in themselves.[39]

Fuller, then, in talking about the infinite being of the individual, its self-determining nature and relation to a larger whole, is drawing on Kantian and post-Kantian notions. This marks a different conception of the basis and nature of individuality from that to be found in the Lockeians, but it does not involve, at any rate in Fuller's case, any difference in the conception of the fundamental rights which individuals must have in order to realize their nature. She endorses fully the type of freedom and equality demanded for all men in the American and French Revolutions, and wants it extended to women. Thus women must have equal political rights, and in respect of civil rights she emphasizes particularly the importance of woman's right to hold property on equal terms with men, and her right to enter any occupation or profession she wishes, whether it be that of sea-captain or politician.

The ground of the claim to equal rights is, as we have seen, that woman is in her deepest nature an individual exactly like man – an individual soul, as Fuller calls it. This soul is of infinite value in woman as well as in man, and the basic conditions of its development and fulfilment are the same for both. These are the rights to inward and outward freedom. Outward freedom consists in the material conditions, the civil and political rights, to form one's own life; inward freedom in the inner achievement of the soul's self-determination through its actualization in the world.

Like Wollstonecraft, however, Fuller pays full respect to the traditional functions of woman in the home as wife and mother.[40] She supposes that most women will remain within the inner circle of home. But this work must not be drudgery, occupying the whole of life, but must be only a part of life, so that a woman is more than wife and mother and is recognized and respected as a being of equal worth with her husband. Such equality will show itself in the first place in a household partnership, in which mutual esteem and practical kindness are expressed through the one partner's function as provider and the other's as house-keeper. In the second place it will show itself in an intellectual companionship or friendship. This does not require a community of employment or an identical occupation, but rather a harmony in difference which produces a community of inward life and perfect esteem. Finally, equality in marriage will show itself in a religious unity, a pilgrimage towards a common shrine. The function of mother, Fuller particularly singles out, calling it a sacred one, and seeing its duties as being the better fulfilled for the free development of the mother's personality.[41]

Fuller's emphasis is on the necessity for woman not to be restricted by these roles. In accordance with her infinite nature she must transcend them by being more than mere wife and mother, and for this she must have the right to expand, to develop her capacities in any direction, to learn to stand on her own feet, to be self-dependent. Like Wollstonecraft, she considers the possibility that when given this freedom, women will not achieve very much. But she holds that superiority of achievement in competition with men is not important; far more important is that women should be acknowledged to have a mind that needs developing and furthermore a mind that needs developing for its own sake, for the infinite worth that it contains. Thus she denies that there is any good in acknowledging that woman has a mind to develop, when the value of this mind is said to lie in her becoming a better and fitter companion for her husband. As a result of her self-development she will indeed be a better companion; but her end is not to be a wife and exist in this specific relation, for she is an end in herself, transcending all relations.

Although Fuller makes the essential feminist claim that in respect of woman's fundamental nature she has a human and not a sexual nature, she has at the same time a strong conception of the destiny of woman as woman, that is to say as a human being modified by a female nature. Thus she says that in giving women their freedom to develop, men have no need to fear that women will wish to be and become like men. Just as the moon has her own sphere, her own strength and beauty, so does woman. Woman has her own special genius which, she says, is electrical in movement, intuitive in function and spiritual in tendency. It is more in woman's nature to inspire creative work than to create it herself. The infinite soul in its feminine form has a tendency to flow, breathe, and sing rather than to complete a work. Male and female represent two sides of a great radical dualism; yet each side is perpetually passing into the other.[42] This conception of woman's nature contains the central elements on which anti-feminist writers base their claim that in accordance with her emotional, passive and receptive nature woman should have an appropriate material sphere in the home, and should not be allowed to enter the male spheres of civil and political society. Fuller entirely rejects the argument from woman's nature to the denial of woman's rights; the argument fails to acknowledge woman to be a soul of infinite value. The right of men to freedom is based only on this value; hence women possessing the same value must have the same rights.

Fuller stresses particularly the need for woman to be shaken out of her traditional dependence on man in order to become self-reliant, and so realize her value as a free and independent being. It is for this that women need a much greater range of occupation than they have previously had. Women have lived too much for others and not enough for themselves, for the value inherent in them. Hence they appear like overgrown children, not self-dependent beings of worth and dignity.[43]

In some final comments Fuller moves away, as I said, from the conception of the self-determining individual to the idea of a

29

larger whole of which individuals are parts. This larger whole she curiously enough calls Man, when she means Humanity. This whole has only one soul, and one body, and an injury to a part is an injury to the whole. The full development and accomplishment of the whole requires the full development of its parts. The whole is differentiated into the basic dualism of masculine and feminine to which correspond the further dualisms of energy/harmony: intellect/love: power/beauty. Hitherto in the history of Humanity the masculine side of the whole has been most developed, but it is now the turn of the feminine principle to receive its full development. Then Man and Woman will be able to regard each other as brother and sister, pillars of one porch, priests of one worship which is the whole that Humanity constitutes.[44]

This, of course, is not exactly an individualist doctrine. A fundamental difficulty which this conception presents for one who attaches the greatest value to individuality, a difficulty which will be taken up later in regard to socialist theories, is that if the individual is in himself merely a part of a larger whole, he cannot also be an infinite being and end in himself. Or rather if he is an infinite being, he cannot be this as an individual human being. There must be an infinite Life, a Universal Mind, which realizes itself in and as the mind of particular human beings. To say this is to abandon the individualist theory altogether, for particular human beings no longer have worth in themselves, but only as they are vehicles for the realization in them of this higher or larger life.

John Stuart Mill (1806–1873)

The major classic of the individualist school in the nineteenth century is undoubtedly J.S. Mill's work *The Subjection of Women*. J.S. Mill writes from a utilitarian standpoint, and something must be said as to the nature of this standpoint and its relation to the individualist school. Indeed the utilitarian philosophy has been very much under attack in contemporary thought for its lack of individualism.[45] Yet there can be no doubt, firstly, that the classical utilitarianism of Jeremy Bentham, James Mill and his son J.S. Mill was strongly individualist in the conception of the social order and individual rights that it espoused. It is in the general justification for such rights that utilitarianism differs from the position of Locke, Rousseau or Kant, and adopts a standpoint which may be said to be anti-individualist. And secondly, J.S. Mill introduced major modifications in the utilitarian philosophy that he inherited from Bentham and his father, and these consisted in a reorientation of the basis of the theory in an individualist direction.

Bentham originally espoused and developed the utilitarian doctrine quite specifically as an alternative to the Lockeian natural rights school. The existence of natural, as distinguished from civil, rights, he thought an absurdity. The underlying difficulty in the natural rights theory has already been discussed in connection with the Kantian development of it. In relation to utilitarianism the same difficulty can be expressed much more simply. For the natural rights theorist the good is the freedom of each individual to do what he wants without being interfered with by others. Although the rightful freedom of each is limited by the equal freedom of others, the problem of a lack of harmony between the rightful wants of each individual remains. A set of secondary moral principles is necessary to resolve such conflicts by determining more specifically each individual's rightful entitlement. But there is considerable difficulty in producing a uniquely convincing set of such principles. Utilitarianism proposes to remove the difficulty by denying that the basic good is the freedom of the individual to do what he wants. Instead the utilitarian principle, as formulated by Bentham, affirms that the only thing that is good in itself is pleasure and the avoidance of pain and the only evil is pain and the absence of pleasure. Everything else is good or bad only as a means to the production of pleasure or the avoidance of pain.[46]

The proper end of action on this view is to maximize the surplus of pleasure over pain for all sentient beings. With respect to man those social and political arrangements are most desirable which satisfy this criterion. In itself this principle, often called the greatest happiness principle, says nothing about the freedom, worth or rights of individuals. Indeed for Bentham there is no radical distinction to be made between the human being and animal species generally. Human beings are of value, not because

31

they are free, rational agents or ends in themselves, but because they are capable of the generation of units of pleasure, which alone is good in itself. Thus there is no value to be attributed to freedom per se, and one cannot say in the same way as Wollstonecraft or Fuller, that human beings are fundamentally of equal worth. The sense in which on Bentham's view all men are equal is that in which equal units of pleasure are to be counted equally in whomsoever they occur.

Nevertheless Bentham has an argument for individual freedom and equal rights which makes him a major proponent of the individualist social and political theory of the liberal school. This argument holds that while the criterion of good action is the maximization of happiness as a whole, taking into account all those affected by the proposed acts or arrangements, yet each individual naturally seeks to maximize his own happiness. Bentham does not believe that each will realize the general happiness by pursuing his own without more ado, for then no general social arrangements would be necessary at all. There is no natural harmony of interests. Yet this harmony can be produced artificially through social and political arrangements within which individuals are to pursue their interests. These arrangements involve a system of equal rights to private property, freedom of contract and of occupation, together with equal political rights, of an identical nature with the ones advocated by theorists who ground their advocacy in a belief in natural rights or the inherent value of individuals.

The reason why the greatest happiness principle requires the same type of freedom and equality for Bentham as that which Lockeians and others demand, is because he believes that allowing a degree of freedom for individuals to pursue the satisfaction of their wants without interference by others is the most effective way of maximizing the production of the means of happiness. Thus a system of rights to acquire and exchange property are fundamental to a general system of happiness. That these rights must be equal Bentham more or less assumes on the basis of individuals' empirically equal capacity for happiness. But this is not an equal right to the means of happiness, since the freedom of acquisition of such means and security of possession preclude it.[47]

J.S. Mill, brought up in this philosophy, became dissatisfied with the conception of the individual personality and the nature of one's ends which it involved. In particular his thought reverted to the view that attributes worth to a human being on the basis of his freedom and rationality. In his essay *On Liberty* the important value is that of self-determination, the choosing of one's own life and values for oneself. He calls this the good of individuality, and identifies it as an integral element in happiness.[48] On this view the condition of happiness for individuals is the actualization of their self-determining nature, and this makes his conception in its fundamental elements much more like those of the individualist writers already discussed.

At the same time Mill alters radically the conception of the equality of human beings and the notion of justice present in the Benthamite philosophy. On Bentham's view justice is the maintenance of that arrangement of equal civil and political rights that is for empirical reasons productive of the greatest happiness. Mill holds on the contrary that an essential element in justice is the equal right of individuals to happiness, and that this fundamental equality of human beings is to be understood as written into the utilitarian principle itself. It is not necessary to follow Bentham in trying to find empirical reasons for equal rights; the equal value of human beings, from which equal rights can be directly derived, is part of the meaning of the utilitarian principle.[49] Whether this is at all a coherent modification of the utilitarian principle, which is still supposed to affirm that pleasure alone is the good and pain the evil, may well be doubted. But we need not consider the matter here. We have established that whatever else Mill's formal adherence to the Benthamite principle may mean, it is to include the notion that individuals in respect of their rational freedom are of inherent worth and dignity.

Let us now turn to Mill's application of these ideas to the woman question. Mill tells us that he had accepted the claims of the feminist position from his youth onwards, when he first learnt to think on social issues under the guidance of his father and Bentham.[50] Bentham, indeed, accepted woman's claim to equality with man in civil and political spheres, although he published nothing on the matter. J.S. Mill was influenced also on this question by Harriet Taylor, who later became his wife. She herself published an essay, *The Enfranchisement of Women*, in the *Westminster Review*.[51] Mill wrote *The Subjection of Women* after his wife's death and in accordance with what he felt were her views on the subject.[52]

In *The Subjection of Women* Mill states that he is concerned to show that 'the existing relations between the sexes, the legal subordination of one sex to the other is wrong in itself, and now one of the chief hindrances to human improvement, and that it ought to be replaced by the principle of perfect equality admitting no power or privilege on the one side nor disability on the other.'[53] We see here at once the combination of the utilitarian concern for consequences with the non-utilitarian emphasis on the inherent injustice of inequality.

It is, of course, an equality of *legal* right, and not an equality of material position and occupation, with which Mill is concerned. He admits that the mass of feeling is against such equality, but insists that this opposition rests on feeling and not on reason, although being all the stronger for this fact. The feeling for inequality, he says, derives from the generality of the practice in the history of mankind. It is felt that what has been established for so long must have good effects. But, Mill claims, the subordination of women rests solely on the law of the strongest. Female subordination is a species of slavery. Originally it took the form of force. It has since become much milder in the course of the general movement of civilization from dependence on force to dependence on consent, and from a society of privilege to one of equality. Despite this increased mildness, subjection on the one side and privilege on the other remain, and the practice stands out as an isolated fact in modern social institutions. The modern world is distinguished by the fact that in it human beings are not born to their place in life, but are free to employ their faculties to improve their lot. Freedom of individual choice is the great modern principle and produces the best consequences for society. Yet being born to a particular place, and not freedom, is woman's lot still. From this discrepancy between the practice of sexual inequality and the general social practice of equality Mill concludes that there must be a prima facie case against the acceptability of the former.[54]

Mill holds that one cannot argue in justification of the present

inequality that the nature of the two sexes has adapted them to
their present functions, for we do not know what women would
be capable of under another system. Like Wollstonecraft, Mill
argues that what is now called the nature of women is an artificial
thing, the result of forced repression in some directions and
unnatural stimulation in others. In general our understanding of
the influences which form human character is very deficient. It is
often assumed that what human beings are now, they have a
natural tendency to be. But this is obviously false. To throw light
on the issue we must study the laws of influence of circumstances
on character. Only those differences could be taken to be natural
which could not possibly be artificial, a residuum after the
deduction of every characteristic of either sex which can be
explained by circumstance. No one has this knowledge yet.[55]

Mill concludes that under present conditions we cannot say
that we know women at all. Indeed those in a position of subordination, who thus live for others, are least likely to express their
true characters to their masters. For this purpose women must be
encouraged to write about themselves. Above all they must have
the freedom to reveal and express what they are and what they are
capable of doing. If women are given their freedom, and they
achieve little, then so be it. Nobody, he says, asks for protective
duties and bounties in favour of women. It is the general opinion
that the natural vocation of woman is that of wife and mother.
Those who wish to prevent women from having opportunities for
engaging in other activities must believe that women would not
marry and bear children, unless they were compelled to do so by
being excluded from other careers. Mill does not believe that
women will fail to fulfil their traditional functions. Men opposed
to equality between the sexes do not really believe it either, he
maintains; they are afraid rather of marriage on equal terms.

Mill has thus established a presumption in favour of equality
between the sexes derived from an appeal to the accepted general
principles for men, namely that a just society involves an
acknowledgment of fundamental equality between them. He
ought in fact to go on to demonstrate that the basis of the claim to
equality between men applies to women also. But he has done
this only by denying that we know that women are made for subordination, and have a nature to serve as wife and mother. This

35

establishes a presumption in favour of their being like men capable of a wide range of activities. But as we have seen in respect of the ideas of Wollstonecraft and Fuller, the important argument is not that women have a capacity to engage in a wide range of activities, but that they are free rational agents capable of directing themselves in their lives. The right to freedom of activity and career follows from their nature and right as free beings. Merely to say that women possibly or probably have the capacity for such activity does not establish their right.

The trouble with Mill's argument is that it does not bring out the basis for the claim of equality in respect of men and so does not apply it clearly to women. This is because he officially holds the position, as we have seen, that the sole criterion of the good is utility, the maximization of happiness, and so he is inclined to be committed to the view that he must demonstrate the beneficial consequences of allowing women freedom. At the same time, as I have argued, he holds that equality is written into the meaning of the utility principle. As a result he assumes that equality is a basic requirement without being clear as to what equality rests upon.

However, Mill's real arguments for equality come in the final section of the book. His earlier sections are devoted to showing that there is subordination, that it is contrary to the dominant belief in equality and that arguments for treating women as a special case to whom equality does not apply have no validity. He proceeds to specify what the new position of equality for women would involve, all the time assuming that equality is just and inequality unjust. In the first place the marriage contract must be changed, and founded on the equality of married persons before the law. Such equality is not a sufficient condition for a full and just equality between the sexes, but is a necessary condition. It is a condition of happiness in family life, and without it the everyday life of mankind cannot be a school of moral cultivation. The only society that can fulfil such a function is a society of equals. Previous moralities were fitted to the relation of command and obedience: these were the morality of submission, and the morality of chivalry and generosity. At present the family is a school of despotism. As a school of equality it would involve an exercise of virtues that would fit its members for all other associations.[56]

Mill accepts that some men now, through love, live their family life in accordance with the morality of equality, but laws and institutions need to be adapted to bad men, not to good. Men must not be trusted with absolute power. It is argued that one person must rule in the family as in the state. But, Mill says, it is not true that in all voluntary associations between two persons, one must have the power of decision, and cites commercial partnerships as examples. In matters requiring quick decisions a division of power will be sensible, while changes of system or principle should require the consent of both parties. Yet Mill recognizes that the real practical division of affairs will greatly depend on the comparative qualifications of the couple. The fact of being older and of being the provider of the means of support for the family will in most cases give the advantage to the man. Inequality in this form does not depend on the law of marriage, but on the existing general conditions of society.

Once again we find the individualist feminist argument leading to an acceptance of the material structure of the family much as it was. Mill envisages the continuation of the common arrangement by which the man earns the family income and the wife superintends the domestic expenditure. In bearing the children and looking after their education, he says, the wife in fact contributes more to the common life. For the wife to go out to work would not usually relieve her of these tasks, but only prevent her from performing them properly. Hence it is not desirable that the wife should contribute by her labour to the household income. As was the case with Wollstonecraft and Fuller, Mill argues that it is the power of earning her own living that is essential to the dignity of a woman. If she is well protected and enjoys equality in marriage, she does not need to labour as well. When a woman marries, she chooses a profession, that of household management and the rearing of children. But there ought not to be anything to prevent exceptional women from pursuing a vocation even if they are married, provided due provision is made for the performance of household duties.[57]

The necessary legal equality between the sexes would, as a matter of course, involve the married woman's retention of a full right in her property and earnings. It would involve, further, the right to enter any profession or occupation. Women's legal disability in this respect, Mill thinks, really has the design of maintaining their subordination in the family. The argument is put forward that women are incapable of the life of the professions, and in so far as they seek a career in them, they depart from the true path of their success and happiness in life. Mill replies to this again that whether or not women are of inferior capacity cannot now be known. It would in any case be irrelevant, since if women are inferior, there would be no need to legislate against them. Fair competition would drive them out. Besides there are women of exceptional ability who would succeed. Mill accepts that there are bound to be fewer women entering the competition for jobs, given their probable preference for domestic life. But this cannot excuse the tyranny of preventing by law competent women from achieving success and contributing to society.

Besides equality of civil rights, women must have the vote. To have a voice in choosing those by whom one is governed is a necessary condition of self-protection due to everyone. Mill then proceeds to argue for woman's *capacity* to enter the public professions on the basis of her demonstrated achievements and human abilities, rather than in terms of what she might achieve given a proper education and development of her faculties. He points to the successes of past women rulers and administrators, and argues that the evidence accords with the accepted view of the practical and intuitive powers of women. Woman's greater concentration on the practical is most probably the consequence, Mill thinks, of her education, in which there is little emphasis on the development of her theoretical powers, and of her experience, in which the management of small but multitudinous detail is required. Even if we assume, he says, what is most improbable, that women's present powers represent their complete abilities, it is clear that they have already the capacity to engage in the public professions.[58]

In a recent article Julia Annas severely criticizes Mill for this section of his argument.[59] She thinks that it is designed to justify reform on the basis of women's natures as they are at present constituted, and that this reveals the essentially reformist nature of Mill's utilitarian position on the woman question. She distinguishes between a reformist and a radical approach: a reformist is one who argues for equality on the grounds that women are now capable of doing what men do, and that to allow women to realize their capacities would make them happier and benefit the whole of society. This is the utilitarian argument. The radical position on the other hand, holds that the subjection of women is inherently unfair even though women now do not have the developed capacities to compete and do not want to compete because they are brought up to be submissive. To change this situation, legal freedom and equality is necessary. But it is not sufficient; a more radical change in society and in the framework of the family is necessary to eradicate the effects of women's traditional inferiority and submissiveness. Mill, she says, confusingly uses both reformist and radical arguments. But when in the section on women's capacities for public life he uses the reformist position, his argument becomes patronizing to women and disastrous for the feminist cause, since it leads through the acceptance of specifically feminine qualities and capacities to the anti-feminist position.

There is, it must be admitted, something unsatisfactory in Mill's position in so far as it purports to justify women's claims to rights on the basis of their actual or probable capacity to engage in the activities of civil and political society. This argument presupposes the equality principle, but does nothing to establish it, or to show that it is applicable to the relations between the sexes. Annas is certainly right in seeing this appeal to capacities, rather than to some justifying principle which upholds the rights of individuals, as deriving from Mill's Benthamite utilitarianism. For if we are not to appeal to the value that lies in individuals as such, then we must appeal to the capacities of human beings to produce pleasure by engaging in this or that activity. This is the reason why we find in Mill such emphasis on this type of argument.

But Annas is quite wrong in thinking that the appeal to capacities in Mill is necessarily to the actual capacities of women rather than to their probable capacities in an altered environment. For it is quite clear that Mill consistently believes that women's capacities under a regime of freedom would be greatly enhanced. The point of his argument in the section that appeals to women's actual capacities is to show that *even if* we rule out the argument from probable capacities, women's actual capacities developed by their present environment are sufficient to justify their claim to political rights.

It follows that Annas is further mistaken in thinking that the argument from capacities is necessarily reformist rather than radical in her sense. The fact is that even those feminists who are not utilitarians, and who argue for the value of individuality, are not radical in her sense: for instance, Wollstonecraft and Fuller. They accept the family, together with the normal woman's role as wife and mother, as it existed. The question raised by Annas's criticism is not the inadequacy of Mill's utilitarianism to accommodate a radical position, but the inadequacy of the individualist theory more generally to do so. As I shall argue shortly, the individualist position does not as such exclude arguments for radical changes in the position of women in society and the family, even if the early individualist feminists did in fact accept the traditional woman's role within an altered legal structure of rights and educational opportunities. That they did so reflects perhaps a sense of the limits of the practicable in the nineteenth century, but is not a necessary implication of individualism.

In the final chapter of Mill's work we find at last that he raises directly the question of the justification for the liberation of women. It is in the form of the utilitarian question: would mankind be better off if women were free? The appeal is to the greatest happiness principle. Will such changes produce a net gain in the quantity of happiness? In the first place, he says, the law of servitude in marriage is not only a monstrous contradiction of all the principles of the modern world, but is productive of the undoubted misery of many women. The modern world in any case has accepted the argument that the practice of servitude does not satisfy the greatest happiness principle. Secondly, in respect of the freedom of women outside the home a great advantage would arise from having the most universal and pervading of all human relations, that between the sexes, regulated by justice. The vast gain to human nature can hardly be exaggerated. All selfish inclinations, according to Mill, are rooted in the present structure of relations between men and women. The boy and adult man are corrupted by their sense of superiority. It is the inevitable result of the development and education of sentiments within domestic life on a basis directly contrary to the first principles of social justice.

We see in these arguments an implicit appeal to the principle of equality as the foundation of justice. The appeal is to the equal worth of human beings and hence their entitlement to equal rights. In no way does Mill attempt to show that the principle of utility involves the equality principle. He takes their identity for granted.

A more clearly Benthamite utilitarian argument is the claim that to give women the free use of their faculties would be to double the mass of mental faculties available for the higher service of humanity, and so be productive of greater happiness. There is a deficiency of competent persons, and the greater competition resulting from women's freedom would provide a stimulus to men. Women must be given the same education as men, and the resulting great expansion of their faculties will increase the quantity and beneficial effect of the influence of female opinion in society generally. The improvement in relations between married partners would also add to happiness. Happiness in married life depends on a union of the thoughts and inclinations of the partners, and this is unlikely to be found where men and women are made so dissimilar by education and character. It is indeed impossible where such dissimilarity is accompanied by mental inferiority. The ideal of marriage involves two persons of cultivated faculties enjoying the best kind of equality, a similarity of powers and a reciprocal superiority in them, so that each may look up to the other.

The greatest gain of all, he concludes, will lie in the private happiness of those liberated, which will result from the difference between a life of subjection and a life of rational freedom. After food and clothing, freedom is the first and strongest want of human nature. The advantages of freedom are as valid for women as they are for men. These lie in the free direction of our faculties as the source of individual happiness. Through this we acquire a sentiment of personal dignity as well as an outlet for our active faculties. Mill states again at this point his view that a sufficient exercise of these faculties, and so a sufficient expression of most women's freedom and dignity, is provided by the care of a family and the management of a household.[60]

In these final remarks Mill reverts closely to the non-utilitarian individualist conception. The value of freedom is still expressed in terms of its relation to happiness, but the freedom and dignity of the individual are seen as integral parts of happiness, and not as means to an independent end. It is through self-direction that an individual acquires dignity, that is to say his worth as a human being. This sense of worth, or self-respect, is a necessary element in happiness. Implicit in this claim is the idea that the worth of human beings lies in their capacity for self-direction. Women should be liberated because they have this capacity. It is not happiness, but worth-dependent happiness that is the goöd.

Later Individualist Feminism

The aim of the organized individualist feminist movement was the attainment of equal civil and political rights for women within the existing structure of liberal and increasingly democratic male society. Great advances in this direction were made in the course of the nineteenth century in respect of such matters as the educational opportunities of women in the secondary schools and universities, and the admission of women to the professions. The laws on divorce, property rights, and control of children in the various countries of Europe and America were all modified to give much greater equality to women. The advance in political rights, however, was very much slower, and more strongly opposed. It was not until after World War I that women's suffrage was secured on a large scale in the Western world. This post-war victory used to be attributed to the recognition of women's contribution to the war effort in industry, and to the increasing anomaly in an egalitarian society of the denial of women's claims to equality with men. However, the idea is now put forward that women were granted the vote because of the conservative value of women voters in opposing the revolutionary pressures stemming from the success of the communists in Russia, and the rise of the workers' parties in the Western democracies.[61]

By the 1920s the aims of the early individualist feminist movement for equal rights had been more or less achieved in much of Europe and America, in so far as equal rights were understood in a formal or legal sense. Within such legal equality there undoubtedly remained inequalities of opportunity for women to develop and realize their talents and to pursue a career in civil or political society. Inequalities of opportunity within a society of equal rights are a consequence of differences in the position of individuals in respect of wealth, education, family and class background, and are experienced by men as well as by women. It may be held that women generally are subject to a far-reaching inequality in so far as their function within the family prevents them from developing their talents and pursuing their careers on equal terms with men. Such a claim would involve the rejection of the view, to be found in the feminists I have hitherto discussed, that women can realize their potentialities adequately within the family sphere. But it would not necessarily involve a rejection of the general framework of individualist ideas. However, it may be argued that if the freedom and equality of human beings involves their equal right to form their own lives in accordance with their capacities, it requires an equality of opportunity to develop and realize those capacities. Otherwise one person's right to freedom is of greater value than another's, and the basic rights are not equal. It is necessary that besides an equality of formal or legal rights, the means to self-realization or to happiness should be equal also.

In the course of the late nineteenth and early twentieth centuries we do in fact find a significant change in liberal ideas associated with the individualist philosophy, which in the manner described above attributes rights to individuals independently of their association with others in a community.[62] The early or so-called classic liberalism, associated with Locke in one form and Bentham in another, allows individuals only rights to compete for the means to achieve their ends within a framework of neutral law. Access to the resources needed to form one's life in accordance with one's plans is to be obtained through individuals' own labour by which they appropriate parts of unowned nature, or by free contract of their labour or possessions with others, or by the free gift of others. Even on Locke's view, however, individuals have rights to be left portions of the earth's surface for them to appropriate in order to satisfy their needs, and after the introduction of money and the creation of political society they have some undefined claims to the attention of the government to their welfare. But his theory does not allow a system of redistributive taxation by the state designed to equalize opportunities. To tax the wealthy for the purpose of equalizing opportunities would be either an unjust interference with the right of individuals to freedom, as in Locke, or an attack on their security which would be productive of quantities of pain insufficiently compensated for by the gains to the poor from redistribution, as in Bentham.

The new liberalism seeks to justify individuals' basic equal right to that quantity of resources necessary to attain their ends. It claims not to depart from the basic value of individual freedom in so doing. If human beings have an equal right to freedom, then it cannot be just that some people, because of their access to the means of freedom, have a greater chance of realizing their ends. Hence the equal right must be understood as an equal right, at least at the outset, to the means of freedom.[63]

It is, however, doubtful whether the argument for an initial equal distribution of resources is compatible with the individualist position. For if there is an initial right to equality of resources, it must be the case that the resources are in the first instance collectively owned and available for general distribution on the basis of needs. Thus implicit in this new liberalism is a collectivist rather than an individualist view. To emphasize these implications is to move away from anything recognizable as liberal individualism in a socialist direction. The difficulty lies in the discrepancy between the collectivist presupposition regarding the ownership of resources, and the continued affirmation of individual freedom as a basic value. For the collectivist presupposition treats the economic activity of individuals, through which the means to freedom are produced, as essentially available for all to benefit from, and hence not the individual's own activity at all. The freedom of individuals to do what they like with what is justly theirs without being interfered with by others is denied.

It is not necessary to pursue these issues further here. It is sufficient to note that this shift in ideas is often presupposed in criticisms of classic nineteenth-century individualist feminism, after its victory in the 1920s. Although in Western countries women received higher education in much larger numbers, although they entered all forms of activity in civil society, and although they had the vote on equal terms, the primary vocation for most women continued to be in the home as wife and mother. If they worked after marriage and with a family, it was generally considered that home and family should come first and a career second. In politics women voted along traditional party lines with their menfolk and only a minute proportion of active political citizens were women.[64]

Since the early individualist feminists had argued for the desirability of this state of affairs as the end-product of liberation, it may appear hardly surprising that women's life-activity had changed so little despite the great efforts that had been made to achieve equal rights. Those who sought equal rights had not aimed to change woman's function in the family. With the rebirth of the movement for women's liberation in the 1960s the older individualist feminists came to be criticized severely from this standpoint. The view came to be accepted that equality for women meant equal opportunity and status in civil and political society, and that henceforth the primary life-activity of women must lie in those spheres and not in the family. If the family is to continue to exist at all, it must take second place for women as it does for men. But to justify this shift in the conception of women's destiny, it is not necessary to repudiate altogether the individualist position. In the first place, the basic value remains, as in the new liberalism, that of the freedom of individuals to realize their ends. In the second place, if the claim is made that women, because of their life as mothers, do not have an equal opportunity with men in civil and political society, and it is held necessary for the state to make arrangements to relieve women of part of this burden (for instance by the provision of nurseries), then such arguments can also be justified within the new liberalism.

It might be thought, indeed, that there is nothing in the basic values of individualist feminism which precludes a thoroughgoing anti-family attitude. On the one hand mothers, as independent individuals seeking to realize their freedom in civil and political society, could consistently within the terms of redistributive liberalism demand of the state that it take responsibility for their children in order to ensure women's equal freedom; and on the other hand the state's responsibility to secure the conditions of freedom for its members could be taken as sufficient grounds to impose on it a duty to care for them from infancy upwards. Once we accept these arguments the family would become a residual affair and no great impediment to the freedom of women. As indicated above, the position appeals to the basic individualist value (even if it contains within itself presuppositions of a non-individualist nature). Thus there is a case for saying that it is possible within the system of values of individualist feminism to argue either for the subordination of family values to women's freedom in civil and political society, or for the liberation of women from the family altogether.

An example of such a transformed individualist feminism is Betty Friedan's work *The Feminine Mystique*. This work played an important part in reawakening among women dissatisfaction with their position in society, and giving new impetus to the feminist movement. Friedan's work is individualist in the sense that her basic value is what she calls the unique human capacity for freedom understood as the capacity of individuals to shape their own future through the pursuit of a career.[65] A civil society in which individuals have the freedom to choose their particular lives for themselves is a necessary condition of the realization of this value. The capacity for and value of freedom applies as much to women as to men. It is neither masculine nor feminine, but human. Thus, if women are to realize their inherent worth as human beings, they must cease to identify themselves with their image as housewives and mothers and pursue careers in civil society.[66]

It is the image of women as essentially feminine, and not human, beings, which is the feminine mystique that Friedan sets out to attack. The image is cultivated, she thinks, throughout women's education and in the media, and is associated with a life as wife and mother. Women are directed by these influences not to think of themselves in the same way as men do, and not to compete with men in civil and political careers. They are to fulfil themselves at home through their sexual relation to their husbands and in the production and rearing of babies. Such a domestic life, Friedan argues, does not permit women to satisfy their basic need to grow and fulfil their potentialities as human beings. She emphasizes the frustration thereby produced in women, especially in those whose personalities have been most developed through higher education. An immense effort has been made, she says, by the cultural institutions of the country to give women prestige in their roles as wives and mothers, to persuade them that their nature can be realized in these roles. But this effort is a failure. Through education women have outgrown the role of housewife. It is impossible for them to create a sense of their identity in a life which, because of its unstructured and repetitive nature, provides no basis for the activity of forming and developing oneself. Women, then, Friedan argues, must reject the housewife image. But this rejection does not require them to give up husband, home and children. They do not have to choose between marriage and a career. Their activity outside the home, however, must not be a mere stop-gap; it must be a serious career, part of a plan for a whole life, and of real value to society. Friedan recognizes, of course, the practical problems involved in combining a family with a serious career. But her general idea is that a woman's family must be conceived and ordered as part of her life-plan, of which a major part is the career. Babies must be planned accordingly, and arrangements for help with minding and rearing them must be made.[67] In her practical work as organizer of the National Organization of Women she has been active in seeking the means – from the provision of nurseries to the securing of legislative changes on equal rights – by which women can fulfil their functions of wife and mother, while realizing themselves primarily, like men, in the development of their capacities in a career.

Friedan's argument seems to bring out the inherent difficulties in the position of the nineteenth-century individualist feminists whom I have discussed in this chapter. They were content to argue that woman's nature as a free, self-forming being could be adequately realized within her traditional roles in the family, which should be seen as a career equivalent to the careers of men in civil and political society. Friedan shows that, ironically, in order to convince women, and especially educated women, who now had a formally equal status with men in society, that their freedom was compatible with a purely family life, the cultural institutions of the country had to give renewed life to the image of woman, not as a human, but as feminine, on the basis of which her freedom had originally been denied.

47

2 Socialist Feminism

Introduction

Individualist ideas in their classic form had hardly received their full development, and the corresponding individualist social and political order had hardly become established in Europe and America, before an antagonist in the form of socialism sprang into being. From the beginning socialist thinkers were for the most part also feminists, for they conceived the conditions for the liberation of man to be at the same time the conditions which would liberate woman from her subjection to man. The major socialist thinkers of the nineteenth century espoused the women's cause in a way that, apart from J.S. Mill, the major theorists of individualism did not. Women themselves had to do the work of applying individualist conceptions to their own nature and position in society. But in respect of socialism this work had already been done for them by the men who originated the socialist ideas. Hence most of the feminists to be discussed in this chapter are men.

The reason for this greater partiality of socialism for the women's cause lies undoubtedly in the attitude of the socialists to the family.[1] Since there is to be under socialism no private property for the family to own and pass on to subsequent generations, there will be no need to rear children privately and consequently no need for women to be tied to the home. Although, as I have argued above, there is no logical necessity for individualism to commit itself to the traditional family in some form, nevertheless individualism has generally supported the family as the natural counterpart to individualist values in respect of property and personality. It has thus been disinclined to allow women to escape from the home and has led feminists of the individualist persuasion not to associate women's freedom with liberation from the domestic life.

Socialism does not consist of a unique and coherent body of doctrine, which can be set down in a limited number of points.[2] But neither is it impossible to generalize on the subject. The early socialist theorists of the beginning of the nineteenth century were united by a conviction that a social order, in which individuals were allowed and encouraged to compete with each other for access to resources and in which they were restrained only by the negative freedoms of personal and property rights, was bound to lead to misery and recurrent economic crises on a large scale. They were agreed that such an order must be replaced by a system of production and exchange which would do away with poverty and exploitation through a redistribution of resources on the basis of equality. They differed, however, on the question of the organization of this alternative order, and also as to the ethical ideas on which the demand for equality and the new order was based. Indeed not all of those who called themselves or were called socialists were unequivocally anti-individualist in their fundamental conceptions, or against some form of private property in the means of production. There are those who, like Hodgskin[3] or Proudhon,[4] believed in the right of the labourer to the full product of his labour, and denied only that it was permissible for one person to own the means of labour of another. The view that a man has a right to the means of his labour is of course the basis of the individualist right to private property. It is used to deny the legitimacy of apparently free contracts which lead to the accumulation of wealth in the hands of the few and to the acquisition of control of the labourer's means of production through which his product is expropriated. It is socialist in the sense of being radically anti-capitalist. Nevertheless, the adherents of this position remain closer to the individualist roots of socialism, and it is relevant to note that, among socialist writers, Proudhon was the staunchest supporter of the family and the most vigorous anti-feminist.

In the works of the early socialist theorists notable expressions of a feminist position are to be found in Charles Fourier, and in William Thompson, a follower of the better-known Robert Owen but in fact a more able theorist than Owen. In this chapter I shall discuss briefly the general socialist, as well as specifically feminist, ideas of these two writers before proceeding

49

to the thought of the major socialist theorist of the nineteenth century, Karl Marx, and the major work of socialist feminism of the nineteenth century, *The Origins of the Family, Private Property and the State* by Friedrich Engels.

William Thompson (c. 1785–1833)

William Thompson was a supporter of the movement for co-operative association led by Robert Owen.[5] Owen could hardly be said to have much by way of a general theoretical position justifying his advocacy of cooperation, and Thompson sought theoretical support for his views from the, at first sight, unlikely source of Benthamite utilitarianism. Since Thompson is no fool and since his use of Bentham is not absurd, it is, as suggested in the last chapter, reasonable to doubt the individualist nature of Bentham's fundamental position.

Bentham undoubtedly uses his fundamental position, with the help of certain empirical assumptions, to justify an individualist social and political order. But if the same fundamental position can be used to justify the opposite order, Bentham cannot be an individualist through and through. It will be recalled that the good for Bentham consists in the maximization of the aggregate of utility which is itself understood as pleasure and the absence of pain. Bentham's justification of individualism consisted in the claim that men's freedom from interference by others was more productive of the means of pleasure than anything else, and that although there was a diminishing marginal utility of resources which would in itself justify their distribution approximately equally, the insecurity of property that would result from effecting the redistribution would produce an overbalance of pain. Thompson accepts the argument for equality and denies the argument from insecurity. He holds that human beings are more or less equal in their capacity for happiness, and this creates a presumption that resources should be distributed equally if aggregate utility is to be maximized. But he also claims that Bentham's arguments in respect of insecurity apply only in an individualist and competitive society. Such a society does not express the true nature of human beings or the true source of their major pleasures. It would be sufficient to change society into a system of cooperative production associations and to educate individuals in accordance with the values of the new society to change altogether the calculus of pleasures. The major source of pleasure in human beings lies, for Thompson, in their sympathetic or benevolent feelings. The immense accession of happiness from the reflected pleasures of sympathy is, he says, hardly to be described. It increases the quantity of happiness more than a thousandfold. Thus although at present human beings seek their happiness in individualist types of activity and selfish pursuits, it is the social system which forces them into this mode of conduct. Given the fecundity of the sympathetic feelings, a far more profitable system is one of cooperative production in which individuals produce for each other and enjoy the pleasures resulting from their contribution to the pleasures of others. Bentham's argument from insecurity of property is thus irrelevant. There will be no private property, and hence no question of redistribution. Resources being possessed in common by members of the cooperative association will be distributed equally in accordance with human beings' equal capacity for happiness.[6]

Thompson became exercised by the woman question as a result of reading one paragraph to be found in the *Essay on Government* by the orthodox Benthamite utilitarian James Mill. In this paragraph James Mill argues that there is no need to grant political rights to those persons whose interests are indisputably included in the interests of others who have such rights. On this basis he dismisses the claims of women to rights.[7] Thompson's book is marked by an intense indignation at Mill's attitude, arising particularly from the fact that Mill's general argument for rights for men is based on the Benthamite assumption of human selfishness and acquisitiveness, and not on any belief in the benevolence or sympathy of mankind. How then, he asks, can Mill make women depend for the satisfaction of their interests on such beings? In attacking Mill, Thompson sets out to show that in terms of Mill's own arguments women must be entitled to an equality of rights. Yet he makes it clear from the beginning that even if women were to acquire formally equal rights in existing individualist society, they would not obtain thereby that equality in the means of happiness which is the fundamental right of each person. Women in individualist and competitive society would be disadvantaged, firstly by their inferior strength and secondly by their periodic withdrawal from the competition for the purposes of child bearing and rearing.[8]

Thompson's most general arguments against Mill's denial of rights to women, which are at the same time of most relevance to his own socialist conception of women's due place in society, are firstly that for˜one person's interest to be included in that of another, that is to say for there to be a real identity of interest between two persons, it is necessary that a perfect equality of position and power should exist between them. For where there is no power of one over the other, there is nothing to prevent the education of their natural benevolence and rationality to a grasp of the truth that their mutual interest lies in the promotion in everything of the real happiness of each other. Where an inequality of power and position exists, as between men and women in the society justified by Mill, the interest of one, Thompson thinks, is clearly different from that of the other, and hence, if either needs the protection afforded by the possession of rights, both do. Secondly, Thompson argues that even where the required equality exists, there would be no case for saying that one party should not have the same rights as the other party, for a general condition of an individual's happiness is that he should be in a position to regulate his own life for himself, and not be dependent on another's benevolence. An equality of rights is a necessary condition of such independence.[9]

Perfect equality is attainable only in the future cooperative society, but Thompson argues very strongly that women, in order to improve their position and begin to raise themselves in preparation for their enjoyment of full equality in the future, must liberate themselves from their present domestic slavery and demand an equality of civil and political rights in competitive society.

The future cooperative society will complete and ensure forever perfect equality and entire reciprocity of happiness for men and women. It will consist of a federation of smaller associations in which men and women will cooperate together for mutual happiness, their possessions and means of enjoyment being equally the property of all, individual property and competition being forever excluded. The great and especial benefit to women of this society will be their liberation from dependence on their husbands. The whole wealth of the community will be available to support women, as it will be to support any man, and the association as a whole will be responsible for the education and support of children. The husband will thus lose that power over his wife, which he always has in individualist society as a result of his greater control over the family's income and wealth, through which he obtains an indirect domination in the privacy of domestic life, even though women may possess formally equal rights. To enjoy equal happiness with men, to associate with them on terms of perfect equality, it is necessary for women to be equally useful to the common good, to engage in an equally useful application of all their faculties of body and mind. Men and women will then enjoy mutual esteem and the highest degree of happiness.[10]

This last point implies that the rights of individuals to the means of happiness should be proportionate to their contributions to the common good. Indeed Thompson says that, although women may contribute fewer products to the association in direct labour, they contribute as much as men when their child bearing and rearing functions are taken into account.[11] Thus there is some confusion in Thompson's mind as to whether the individual's basic right is to an equality of the means of happiness, each person's capacity being the same, or only to a quantity of means proportionate to a person's contributions to the common good. In the case of men and women as a whole Thompson thinks that the two criteria will produce the same egalitarian result, but they obviously need not do so.

Furthermore, in claiming that women's contribution to the cooperative association will be equivalent to men's, Thompson tells us that women will continue to be responsible for the rearing of children, and it is not clear how this is to be understood. Since he insists that children are to be educated and provided for by the whole association, it might be supposed that the rearing of children is to become a public responsibility, and women would be involved only as public nurses and teachers. But he could mean that the young children will remain within the family and be the immediate responsibility of their mothers. Only, since mothers would be supported by the association and not by their husbands, this would in effect make them public servants within the family home.

It should be evident from this account of Thompson's thought that while in terms of his ideas on the organization of society he is clearly a socialist and not an individualist, his basic values can be understood as a form of the individualism referred to in the last chapter as the new liberalism. For he comes to argue for the individual's need to regulate his own life, and to be dependent only on himself, and this requires that the ends, which an individual chooses in pursuit of his happiness and for the attainment of which he is entitled to an equality of means with everyone else, must be chosen by himself and not given to him by his collective. No theoretical justification is provided for this important claim, either of the kind we find in J.S. Mill or of a more Benthamite empirical nature – for instance the idea that each individual is the best judge of his own interest and hence must have the freedom to form his life for himself. But the acceptance of it by Thompson reintroduces an element of individualism into his thought at a fundamental level.

I do not intend to imply by these remarks that a peculiar incoherence attaches to Thompson's thought. I have indicated in Chapter 1 unsatisfactory elements in individualism, and I shall indicate again in my final chapter that a complete coherence escapes both individualist and socialist thought.

Charles Fourier (1772–1837)

The Frenchman Charles Fourier also rejects individualist and competitive society in favour of the cooperative organization of production in small associations. At the same time his general framework of ideas, although not explicitly utilitarian, requires similar assumptions. He believes that there is a passional code in human beings which is such that, were society to be organized by reference to it, human beings would discover the satisfaction of their passions in activity which serves directly or indirectly to satisfy the passions of all others also. In present society, this passional code is not followed and human beings find themselves committed to activities which involve the frustration of both their own passions and the passions of others. They are placed in a state of war with themselves and with other men. Thus co-operative production is justified by Fourier in terms of the greater amount of desire-satisfaction or pleasures realized in it.

The passions which Fourier has in mind are by no means all self-regarding ones, but the calculus of pleasure in justifying cooperation does not depend overwhelmingly, as it does for Thompson, on the extraordinary quantities of pleasure to be obtained from the other-regarding feelings of sympathy and benevolence. The greater pleasure productivity of cooperation results, according to Fourier, firstly from the greater efficiency of cooperative production, with the consequence that there will be a larger quantity of wealth available for each person to enjoy. The greater efficiency comes about largely through the elimination of the waste of resources involved in the distributive trades in competitive society. Secondly, through planned production it will be possible to arrange the work programme of individuals so that everyone has a variety of occupations which suits his particular combination of passions or passional code. Hence work will be a direct source of pleasure, and individuals will willingly spend much longer hours in production so that the general wealth of the association will be greatly increased.

Fourier's theory of passionate attraction is thus the basis of his system. Indeed in his view everything in the universe, including the planets, is moved by passionate attraction. In order to know how this works in human beings, we need to know the passions that work in them. There are twelve radical passions forming three categories: (a) the luxurious passions consisting of the five senses, (b) the affective passions of friendship, ambition, love and parenthood, and (c) the distributive or mechanizing passions, the free expression of which is essential for the gratification of the other nine. These are the cabalist, butterfly and composite passions. Cabalist is the passion for intrigue and competition, butterfly is the passion for variety, and composite is the passion for complexity and requires for its satisfaction a mixture of physical and spiritual pleasures. The combined action of the last group would keep the other nine in a state of perfect equilibrium and permit the formation of what Fourier calls the passionate series, the groups which are the basic production units in his ideal community.[12]

The ideal community, then, aims at maximal gratified desire. But individuals' desires are such that, given an appropriately organized environment, the gratification of one individual's desire makes him eminently useful for others. For instance, work in competitive society is unpleasant to the workers who have to be compelled or bribed to work. This is because individuals have to perform only one task or profession, which becomes boring, repetitive and limiting. It fails to satisfy two of the distributive passions, the butterfly and composite ones, by excessive concentration on the other. In the ideal community individuals will continue to specialize in particular professions, but each will practice up to thirty different professions. In these circumstances work will be a delight. It will be so full of gratified desire that the distinction between work and play will have been broken down. Such work realizes the highest form of freedom, which is a compound of physical freedom, by which Fourier means the satisfaction of basic physical needs, and social freedom, by which he means the gratification of passions in an active way. Both physical and social freedom are realized in the same activity, the attractive work which provides for the individual's physical needs and his active social passions at the same time. The society that realizes this freedom completes the destiny of humanity.[13]

Life in the phalansteries, as the cooperative associations which Fourier envisages are called, would be communal but in the way in which hotel living is communal, with private rooms and centralized services. Furthermore, private property and economic inequality would not be altogether abolished. A high minimum subsistence, or level of gratified desire, would be secured to everyone, and production would be cooperative. But individuals would be rewarded according to their labour contributions to the total product, and would also get dividends on their initial capital contributions to the phalanstery. The division of the total product would be such that the larger one's share of the capital the lower would the rate of return on it be. Public affairs would be organized on democratic principles and would become largely a matter of the administration of work, but also of the love affairs of members of the association.

Fourier elaborates the organization of his ideal community with loving and idiosyncratic detail. It is not necessary to enter into this, however, for the purposes of understanding his ideas on the position of women. Fundamental to his views of women is his attitude to the family. The inhabitants of the phalanstery will not live in families. Fourier considers monogamous marriage and the nuclear family to be disastrous institutions both from the point of view of economic efficiency, and from that of a life of gratified desire. As regards the former, the separate life of the family is the cause of enormous and wasteful distribution costs; as regards the latter, monogamy fails to meet the requirement that Fourier lays down for the minimum membership of a group capable of producing gratified desire. This number is three. Furthermore, Fourier believes the erotic impulse to be complex, containing a vast potential for social good. Love is a compound passion, being both spiritual and physical, and cannot be limited to the narrow bounds of marriage. In the ideal community sexual love is the soul and vehicle of universal attraction. Its amorous institutions bind together individual satisfaction and social welfare.[14]

There is thus no barrier to women's full participation in the work and administration of the phalanstery. Indeed women's position in the phalanstery will be the touchstone of its attainment of the highest state, that of Harmony. Fourier believes that women have been ill-treated in all past societies. He holds that there have been seven historical societies prior to the emergence of the ideal. In each historical period there is a pivotal mechanism on which the social order is based. This is always drawn from the passion of love and manifests itself in the relation between the sexes. Thus the fourth period, which he calls barbarism, involves the absolute servitude of women. The fifth period, called civilization, by which he means the society of his day, involves monogamous marriage together with civil liberties for the wife. But this arrangement still constitutes an oppression of women. Women are formed by their education to become wives and mothers. Hence the development of their faculties is governed by the needs of these functions, and their natural sexual impulses as well as other passions which seek fulfilment in complex attractive work, are severely repressed. At the same time, because they depend upon men as husbands to support them, they have to cultivate sexual wiles and charms in order to catch and hold a man. In the process they acquire artificial personalities which men despise. But to judge women by the defective character they display in the period of civilization is absurd. In the final period of Harmony they will surpass men in dedication to work, in loyalty and nobility. In a state of liberty, indeed, women will surpass men in all mental and bodily functions not related to physical strength. Woman's historical inferiority has been due entirely to her oppression by the male who has used his superior strength to impose a repressive and limiting education on her.[15]

Under civilization women are the most exploited group. They live in a state of continual ungratified desire. In industrial work they are restricted to the most menial and degrading tasks, and the only means of subsistence for impoverished women are their charms. This is the consequence of the conjugal slavery that women are forced to accept. Just as Thompson appeals to women to liberate themselves, so does Fourier conjure up the idea of a female Spartacus who will devise a means of raising her sex from its degradation.

According to Fourier the touchstone of progress in society is the improvement in the position of women, the progressive liberation of the physically weaker sex. The best nations are those which have conceded the greatest amount of liberty to women. He puts forward the general proposition that social progress and changes of historical period in the advancement of mankind towards Harmony have been brought about by virtue of the progress of women towards liberty. In short the extension of the privileges of women is the fundamental cause of all social progress. This liberation becomes complete in the phalanstery with the abolition of monogamous marriage and the family. Children will be brought up collectively by particular work groups whose interests lie in this direction. Men and women will continue to have parental feelings of affection for their children, but these will be pure sentiments unmixed with uglier feelings derived from the constraints and repressions of the private family. Liberated from the family and educated like men for the full development of their faculties in attractive work and in love, women will reveal their true capacities in surpassing men.

As noted above, Fourier defines freedom in terms of the gratification of passions. It is freedom from unsatisfied desire. Furthermore, the desires are a natural given, man's passional code, which it is necessary to crack in order to think out the appropriate work and living conditions for complete gratification. Human reason is simply the means whereby this is done. There is here no conception of the individual's freedom as a rational being in the sense of a capacity to form one's own life by setting oneself ends of action. Men and women are essentially complex passionate beings. Although individuals are supposed to participate democratically in the administration of the phalanstery, the whole of life appears as a minutely organized social mechanism for the maximal satisfaction of desires, which themselves are determined by nature, not formed by each individual in the determination of his own life.

There is in Fourier's conception of the human being little of the understanding of the nature of the self and of the conditions of human individuality which informs and indeed provides the rationale for the individualist social and political theory described in Chapter 1. There seems little more reason for calling human beings as conceived by Fourier free, than there is for saying of an animal whose conditions of life ensure the full satisfaction of its natural desires that it is free. Of course, Fourier builds into his conception of men's natural desires a spiritual or rational element. Thus the second category of affective passions contains friendship, ambition, love and parenthood. Such passions are not natural in the sense of arising in the human being unformed by thought or conscious aim, and so unformed by human rationality. Friendship and love are not instinctive desires for association with another, but involve the conscious making of another individual a partner of one's hopes and purposes. They presuppose the capacity of the individual to direct himself in accordance with ends of his own choosing. Without this capacity one would be neither the sort of being that had hopes and purposes for its life which it desired another being to value through bonds of love or friendship, nor the sort of being that could seek to make another a valuer of its life. As for the passion of ambition, it is immediately obvious that it involves the capacity of the individual to set himself ends. Although these rational elements of human activity are presupposed in Fourier's account of the passions, he nevertheless assimilates the passions to instinctive desire, and by failing to recognize the self-directing rational capacity for what it is, he is unable to understand the conditions for its realization.

In the account given above of Thompson's thought it was noted that he included in his utilitarian theory a conception of the human being as an independent self-regulating individual. In this respect, then, he is in advance of Fourier. Nevertheless Thompson's understanding of the self is also unsatisfactory, and it will be helpful to consider briefly the reasons for this, prior to embarking on a survey of the thought of the socialist theorist who aimed to resolve the problems of human freedom and individuality in a much more radical and ambitious way than his socialist predecessors – namely Karl Marx. One of Thompson's basic assumptions, it will be recalled, is that resources, or the means of happiness, are collectively owned and are to be distributed by society to individuals in accordance with the requirement of maximizing utility. Since resources do not simply lie around for the community to distribute as it thinks fit, but are the result of human beings' productive efforts on nature, the assumption of collective ownership requires that all production be organized for the good of the community and not for that of the individual. Thompson's justification for this communal requirement lies in his conception of the effect of sympathy in maximizing pleasure.

Activity directed towards producing pleasure in others is the most pleasure-giving activity for the individual himself. Evidently, however, human beings must continue to have desires for themselves, which may be called primary desires, for otherwise the secondary desires for the pleasure of others would have no means of being satisfied. A desires the pleasure of B, but if B's desires are solely secondary ones they would consist in desiring the pleasure of A who himself desires only the pleasure of B. Primary desires of the individual for himself there must be, but they must be purely consumption desires and not desires to carry on a productive activity. For productive activity, which brings into being the means of happiness, must be directed to the benefit of the whole and not to that of the individual. But this involves an arbitrary and incoherent conception of the self. It is arbitrary because no principles can be adduced to show that primary desires for the self cannot and should not include desires to engage in this or that productive activity. It is incoherent because it means that the individual's productive talents and capacities, the development of which may be the object of his primary desires, must be seen not as belonging primarily to him, but as belonging essentially to the community to be developed and used for its benefit. On this view the independent, self-regulating individual is solely a passive consumer, and not an agent at all.

These difficulties raise directly the question of the social nature of the individual. An opposition is being drawn between the individual and society which, if accepted at all, undermines the clarity and coherence of the socialist position, and forces one to introduce elements from the individualist theory. An attack on precisely this point is a central element in Marx's ethical theory and constitutes a suitable place to begin an account of that theory. Although Marx himself wrote little on the woman question apart from affirming, following Fourier, its importance for the general liberation of humanity, the most important work of socialist feminism of the nineteenth century is that of Marx's collaborator Engels, and an understanding of the basic Marxist doctrine is necessary background to it.

Karl Marx (1818–1883)

In the brief account given above of the Kantian development of individualist thought it was noticed how a division emerged from within the individual's nature between his particular being concerned with his own particular interests and ends, and his moral being directed towards the recognition and pursuit of the equal value of all particular selves. The one inclines the individual to the love of self and the other to the love of equality. This does not appear to be a fully coherent conception of the individual's nature.

In his early writings Marx developed a critique of individualist throught directed at this division in the self and used it as the basis for his very different conception of the relation of the individual to the moral and social whole. The clearest formulation of this critique is to be found in an essay entitled *On the Jewish Question*. In this essay Marx is responding to an article by a fellow radical called Bruno Bauer who claimed that there were no grounds for the *political* emancipation of the Jews, since the emancipation of the Jews was a *religious* problem. Bauer's solution to the problem requires the emancipation of man from religion, so that all become undifferentiated men and citizens. For Marx such a purely religious emancipation of man is superficial because it is the peculiarity of the modern liberal and democratic state that it emancipates men politically by recognizing them on the political level as undifferentiated and equal men and yet leaves their real identity as members of particular groups, classes or religions unchanged. The member of a democratic state can be liberated politically and yet not be free and equal.[16]

In the rest of the essay Marx examines the reason for this peculiar state of affairs and finds it to lie in the liberal democratic state's annulment of private property as a qualification for citizenship, but its failure to abolish it in reality. The state thus proclaims the equality of man politically, but by leaving the real material life of man in civil society unchanged, it leaves real human inequality untouched. As a result a division is created in man between his private being in civil society and his communal essence which is separated off and posited as belonging in the separate realm of political society. In civil society the individual has rights to do what he likes, to pursue his private ends without interference by others, a right of selfishness. In this material or real sphere men are held together, not by their communal nature, but by their private need to use each other. In the separate political sphere men aspire to the realization of their common good, but because it is the economic man of civil society, and not political man, who is real, it is his interests which will effectively dominate and nullify the ideals of political society.[17]

Marx concludes the essay with a brief statement of the requirements of a full human emancipation. This must involve a reintegration of the abstract citizen with individual material life: the individual, 'as an individual man in his empirical life, in his individual work and individual relationships [must] become a species-being; man must recognize his own forces as social forces, organize them and thus no longer separate social forces from himself in the form of political forces'.[18] This is to say that man's individual forces and activities are really social forces and activities, which he misrepresents and misorganizes as private to himself. The abolition of private property and the separate state would bring about the required reintegration of individual and communal nature, and hence realize the true and essential unity of individual and society.

The doctrine that the individual is the social being, that individual activity is at the same time and essentially social activity, has great advantages over the individualist and socialist doctrines hitherto considered. In respect of individualist doctrines, it immediately does away with the opposition between the particular being of the individual directed to his particular life and his moral being concerned with the common good. There is no essential opposition between the two because the particular individual is really only an expression of the activity of the social whole. Equally it does away with the problem in Thompson's thought arising from the requirement that the productive activity of the individual be directed to the benefit of the whole and not to the ends of the particular self. This difficulty is from the Marxist viewpoint once again a feature of the failure to grasp the inherent unity of individual and social. The particular individual in fulfilling his particular nature relates himself to the satisfaction of other particulars through which the social whole is completed.

According to Marx man alienates himself from his essential social nature by separating his social essence from his particular activity. In the *Economic and Philosophic Manuscripts*, written shortly after *On the Jewish Question*, but not published by Marx, the nature and content of this alienation is explored. Here he develops the idea that the essential human power, which is both individual and social, is labour, understood as a productive and creative activity. By labouring on external nature the individual develops his essential human power and objectifies it in the form of the products of his labour. He is thus related to these transformations of nature as to his own essence. Alienation is the inability to relate to the object and activity of labour in this way. The root of alienated labour lies in the alienation of the worker in the act of production through the sale of his labour to another. The object of the worker's labour is appropriated by another, and the worker is left related, not to his proper object, but to what he can get through the sale of his labour, subsistence wages. His object in his work becomes the purely private, self-interest.[19]

The essential human characteristic is free conscious productive activity, and the individual in engaging in this activity in an unalienated way is realizing his species-essence, giving it an objective form in his products. But each individual contributes only a part of this objectification of essential species-powers. The realization of the whole does not lie directly in each individual but only in the series of productive acts of particular individuals taken together. The realization of the whole is completed only in the series. Thus a particular individual cannot realize the species in himself, but needs this relation to all others to complete it. This is the meaning of the social essence of individual activity: that the value which lies in the individual in respect of his general or essential nature as species-being can be realized only through the relation of his productive activity to that of others, thus making others necessary to the completion of his essence. On this view, in contrast to the individualist idea, the individual has no value in himself, but only as part of the whole, only in so far as the species-powers are being partially realized in him. Marx intends that his theory should be understood to involve the affirmation and complete realization of the values of freedom and individuality, and not their reduction to the status of means to the end of a larger whole. As stated, he sees no opposition between the claims of the individual and the claims of society.

It is well known that Marx does not provide, in either his early or later writings, any account of the institutions and practices through which communist values are to be realized. Marx considers that this task must be left to the revolutionaries themselves to undertake, and that no one in the present could lay down the form of life appropriate to the future communist society. However, there is one obvious way of giving general institutional form to these ideas: as a centrally planned and administered economy, which treats the economy as a whole as a single unit and each individual's labour as part of the whole. Whether such a collectivist economy can be democratically run, we need not consider. The point to be made here is that in such a scheme individuals or groups have no freedom to make productive decisions for themselves. At most they can participate in the collective decisions as to how their productive labour is to fit into the whole.

Collectivism of this kind has in fact been the universal tendency of all Marxist regimes, and indeed it is difficult to see how otherwise the communist idea could be realized on a large scale. Nevertheless, it is possible to treat such regimes as forms of bureaucratic totalitarianism contrary to the essential ideas of Marx himself, because the individual functions in them solely as a subordinate means to the interests of the whole as determined by the central organizations. But according to Marx's ideas on the overcoming of alienation, the individual and society are one, and this, it can be argued, cannot mean the subjection of the individual to the dictates of a centralized bureaucracy. The idea of the unity of individual and society should be understood rather as the view that each individual in his spontaneous self-activity immediately harmonizes with the self-activity of others precisely because in communist society all opposition between individual and society is overcome. Such a view could not possibly be given an institutional expression since any institution is a way of artificially harmonizing the self-activity of individuals. It is in effect the view that in communist society there will be no need for institutional restraints of any kind. This anarchist interpretation of Marx is important for understanding the Marxist element in contemporary radical feminism.

Marx's work on the nature of man's social essence and its alienation dates from the early period of his writing. He does not, however, in his mature work reject these ideas. He is concerned rather with explaining how alienation comes about, and how its overcoming in communism can be achieved. In so doing he develops the materialist conception of history, which it will be necessary to sketch in.

Marx's materialism springs from the need to avoid an idealist interpretation of the above doctrine regarding the social essence of man. An idealist interpretation would make thought, rather than the productive activity itself, the determining factor in the realization of the essentially social nature of man's labour and this could not be reconciled with the idea of man as essentially a producer and not a thinker. His problem is then to give an account of the emergence of the consciousness of man's social nature, and hence of socialism, which is compatible with the primacy of production, and yet does not make of thought a crude and causally unimportant reflection of this productive activity. A view is needed which shows how the social essence is being produced in the world in accordance with man's productive activity, but which allows also for the conscious apprehension of it in man's thought as at the same time a necessary element in its realization. An historically structured social theory is required in which this relation is expressed and the realization of the social essence of man in history accounted for. This is what Marx sets out to provide in his later work. Since Marx does not in this work renege on his conception of the social nature of man, and since this conception is now fully conscious in his thought, he is committed to the view that the world is ripe for the realization of socialism. He needs to show how history is producing out of itself, or how men acting in history are necessarily producing as a result of their labour, the conditions and instruments for the overthrow of alienated society and the establishment of socialism.

The materialist conception of history is succinctly expressed in the *Preface to a Contribution to the Critique of Political Economy of 1859*. He makes the following claims: (1) 'In the social production which men carry on they enter into definite relations that are indispensable and independent of their will'; these he calls relations of production and holds that any particular set of relations of production corresponds with a particular stage of development of men's material forces of production.[20] The latter consist basically of the means of production and labour power. The productive forces require definite production relations for their effective utilization, and by relations of production, Marx means not only and not primarily the relations between workers at the workplace, but the relations involving the control and direction of productive forces, which are essentially in legal form the property relations of production. (2) 'The sum total of these relations of production constitutes the economic structure of society – the real foundation, on which rises a legal and political superstructure and to which correspond particular forms of social consciousness. The mode of production in material life determines the social, political and intellectual life processes in general. It is not the consciousness of men that determines their being, but on the contrary their social being that determines their consciousness.' This statement should not be interpreted to mean that thought is purely a passive reflection of economic processes. Without an appropriate social consciousness the society as a whole, including its mode of production, could not function. (3) 'At a certain stage of their development the material forces of production in society come into conflict with the existing relations of production – or what is but a legal expression for the same thing with the property relations within which they have been at work before. From forms of development of the forces of production, these relations turn into their fetters. Then begins an epoch of social revolution. With the change of the economic foundation the entire immense superstructure is more or less rapidly transformed. In considering such transformations a distinction should always be made between the material transformation of the economic conditions of production, and the legal, political, religious, aesthetic or philosophic – in short, ideological forms in which men became conscious of this conflict and fight it out'. It is a particular social class, whose interest it is to bring about the change in the relations of production, which will enable the further development of the productive forces to occur. But for this to happen the rising class must proceed to a revolutionary transformation of the superstructure, and this itself involves a development of thought appropriate to the emerging form of social being. The proletariat is the class whose interest it is to overthrow capitalism, and socialist theory expresses the consciousness of the proletariat of their condition, their interest in its transformation and in their own essential nature. In the proletariat's revolutionary practice is the social essence of man brought forth in unalienated form. (4) 'In broad outlines we can designate the Asiatic, the ancient, the feudal and the modern bourgeois modes of production as so many epochs in the progress of the economic formation of society. The bourgeois relations of production are the last antagonistic form of the social process of production ... the present formation constitutes, therefore, the closing chapter of the prehistoric stage of human society.'

In constructing his theory Marx had very little to say about the position of women. He took it for granted that socialism would bring about the liberation of women as well as of men, but left it to his collaborator Engels to develop both an historical materialist account of women's subordination in society, and a view of their position under socialism. These ideas were further expressed by another follower of Marx, August Bebel, who will be considered later. Marx's few thoughts on the woman question are to be found in the *Economic and Philosophic Manuscripts*, and echo Fourier's idea that the exact stage of man's advance towards the realization of his true nature can be discerned from the treatment accorded to women in society. 'The immediate, natural and necessary relationship of human being to human being is', Marx says, 'the relationship of man to woman. In this relationship is sensuously revealed how far man has transformed his natural relations in accordance with his social essence. From the character of this relationship we can conclude how far man has become a species-being, a human being, and conceives himself as such.'[21] That is to say, the relation of man to woman – the sexual relation whereby the species is reproduced – is at bottom a part of nature. The actual relation of man to woman in society will reveal how far man has transformed this nature and moved towards the realization of his social essence. That women are to be understood as fully equal species-beings with men goes without saying, and that under socialism there will be nothing to prevent them realizing this social nature alongside men follows from the fact that, together with other forms of private life, the family will be abolished.

It is obvious that an adequate Marxist feminist theory would have to relate changes in the family and in women's position to the general economic transformation of society, and would have to show how the economic changes under socialism would achieve the full liberation of women which Marx is content simply to posit. These tasks Engels undertakes in his work *The Origins of the Family, Private Property and the State*.

Friedrich Engels (1820–1895)

Engels states that according to the materialistic conception of history the determining factor 'in the final instance is the production and reproduction of immediate life'.[22] By this he means both the production of the means of existence and the reproduction of human beings themselves. It is the combination of these two forms of production, the stage of development of labour on the one hand and of the family on the other, which determines the social organization of a particular historical epoch. This appears to make the family a separate or at any rate a distinguishable determining factor of the social whole, as though the family were not itself determined by the mode of production of the means of existence, and as though the exploitation of women were a phenomenon parallel to but not dependent on the emergence of the exploitation of a class of male workers. But this is misleading. On Engels's view, as he develops it, the subordination of women in and through the family first arises, together with the subordination of a slave class, as a result of the emergence of private property, and both will disappear with the disappearance of private property.

Engels begins his account of the origin of the family with some speculations as to a pre-historic state of communism derived from the work of the contemporary American anthropologist Lewis Morgan. The supposition of an original but primitive state of communism is a necessary idea in the Marxist theory as the ground for the notion of man's alienation of his communal nature in private property and subsequent return to it in its fully developed form after the socialist revolution. Marx and Engels seized upon Morgan's work, both for this reason and because of the compatibility of his account of social change with their own materialist conception. Morgan distinguishes two historical periods prior to civilization, those of savagery and barbarism, each of which is further subdivided into three stages according to the progress made by man in the production of food. The details of Morgan's classification need not concern us, but in broad outline under savagery man as hunter and gatherer appropriates nature in its natural form, while under barbarism he begins to transform nature through the herding of cattle and cultivation of plants. Civilization, the form of life to which barbarism leads, consists in the more advanced application of work to the products of nature in the development of industry and art.[23]

The origin and development of the family is to be fitted into this basic schema. Using Morgan's anthropological evidence from North American Indian and Hawaian sources Engels supposes that the original family consisted in a state of group marriage, by which he means a state in which all the members of the group possess one another. This common possession does not exclude temporary pairings, but no restriction is imposed by the group on sexual intercourse. There is not even an incest taboo. The family develops from this original group marriage to the narrowing of those bound in marriage to the single pair. It is supposed that there must first have been a consanguine family, which excludes sexual intercourse only between parents and children, and then a so-called punaluan family, which extends the incest taboo to cover brothers and sisters.[24]

It is a characteristic of all forms of group marriage, including the consanguine and punaluan types, that only the mother of the child is known and not the father. Thus descent can be reckoned only through the female line. This leads to the important claim that in the earliest societies the family organization can be characterized as one in which mother-right is the dominant principle. The existence of such an original period of mother-right identified with the idea of female dominance in society became a matter of ideological importance in some feminist thought. If it could be shown that the apparent universality of female subordination was false, and that on the contrary at an early period of human society women's right predominated, it would follow that the traditional family organization of the period of civilization, monogamy and female subjection, had no claim to being a universal value.

From the punaluan family develops the pairing family, coming into existence on the border-line between savagery and barbarism. It is the characteristic family organization of barbarism. Engels accounts for this transition in terms of the genetic advantages resulting from the exclusion of inbreeding in the pairing family. It emerged in the first place because women desired to free themselves from the promiscuity of group

70

marriage, and subsequently spread successfully through the processes of natural selection. The pairing family binds one man to one woman, but the relation is such that polygamy and occasional infidelity is permitted to men, and the marriage tie can be dissolved without difficulty by either partner. The children continue to belong solely to the mother, and the communistic household of the original group organization remains. Such communistic housekeeping, Engels claims, ensures the supremacy of the women in the house, just as the exclusive recognition of the female parent ensures that women are held in high respect.[25]

With the transition from unrestricted group marriage to the prohibition of marriage between blood relations a new social organization, called the gens, emerges. This involves the grouping of tribesmen into kin of various categories which determine the possible marriage relations. Each gens constitutes a communistic household, and as a marriage within the gens is prohibited, and mother-right continues to predominate, marriage involves the man going to live with the woman's gens. This communistic household in which the women belong to one and the same gens, while the men come from various gentes, is according to Engels the material foundation of the supremacy of women in primitive times. There is nevertheless a sexual division of labour. The men are occupied with hunting and are the main food providers, while the women do the housework. Furthermore there exists a limited private property within the household consisting in the ownership of weapons, household instruments and so on, which subsequently serves as the basis for the great expansion of private property, the destruction of the communistic household and the overthrow of mother-right.

Within the period of barbarism the domestication of animals and the breeding of herds develop, which constitute a new source of wealth and produce entirely new social relations. Engels supposes that the herds must originally have belonged to the gens, but admits that private property in them began at an early period, since at the threshold of authentic history we already find herds separately owned by heads of families.

The development of herding coincides with the invention of slavery. To the barbarism of the lower stage a slave is valueless. There is no surplus product from human labour over and above its maintenance costs. But with the introduction of cattle-breeding, metal-working, weaving, and lastly agriculture, this situation is completely changed. It now becomes profitable to possess other men's labour power, especially as the herds have become the private possessions of the pairing family.

This new private wealth undermined the society founded on pairing marriage and the matriarchal gens. In the pairing family the husband acquires a warrant of paternity, and with the division of labour within the family he provides the food and owns the instruments of labour, and in the case of separation between husband and wife, he takes his instruments while she retains her household goods. Now the man is the owner of the new source of wealth, the cattle, and of the new instruments of labour, the slaves. But according to the custom of that society his children cannot inherit from him. A man's property passes to his nearest relatives in his gens, and as his children are members of his wife's gens and not his own, his possessions would go first to his brothers and sisters and then to his sisters' children. His own children are disinherited.

As the new source of wealth increases it makes the man's position in the family more important than the woman's, and encourages the man to exploit his strengthened position in order to overthrow in favour of his children the traditional order of inheritance. The revolution consists in the overthrow of mother-right by the decree that the offspring of male members of the gens should remain with it, while those of the female members should be excluded by being transferred to the gens of the father. This complete reversal of matrilineal for patrilineal descent Engels calls the world-historical defeat of the female sex. Man takes command in the home and woman is reduced to servitude. She becomes the slave of his lust, and a mere instrument for the production of children. This position, he says, is now gilded over, but has not been abolished.[26]

The establishment of the exclusive supremacy of the man shows its effects first in the formation of the patriarchal family. Its essential characteristic is the organization of a number of persons, both slave and free, into a family under paternal power for the purpose of holding lands and breeding cattle. The perfect type of this family is, according to Engels, that of Ancient Rome.

In the Roman family the wife is delivered over completely and unconditionally to the power of the husband in order to make certain of her fidelity and hence of the paternity of her children. A good contemporary instance of this family type Engels observes in the Southern Slav form. It comprises several generations of the descendants of one father, together with their wives, who all live together in one homestead, cultivate their fields in common, feed and clothe themselves from a common stock, and possess in common the surplus from their labour. This community is under the supreme direction of the head of the house, who acts as its representative in relation to the outside world.[27]

The patriarchal family is a transitional stage in the development of the monogamous family. This latter is the simple married couple without the larger family community. It is based on the supremacy of the man and its express purpose is to produce children of undisputed paternity who can inherit the father's property. It is distinguished from the pairing marriage of the period of barbarism by the much greater strength of the marriage tie which can no longer be dissolved at the wish of either partner. As a rule it is now only the man who can dissolve it and put away his wife. There is also by custom a right of conjugal infidelity belonging to the man but not to the woman. Monogamy, Engels says, is for the woman only.

This is evident from the form the monogamous family takes in classical Greece. Together with his legitimate wife who is entirely subordinate to him, the husband has female slaves in the household who produce children for him. The presence of young beautiful slaves for the man again gives monogamy its specific character of monogamy for the woman only. In the later ancient Greek period we find women limited to definite female tasks of domestic labour, living more or less behind locked doors with no company except that of other women. They never go out without being accompanied, and indoors they are kept under regular guard. Alongside this domestic control of wives there is an extensive system of prostitution, through which women of personality and talent are able to acquire and develop the intellectual and artistic culture by which they surpass the general level of classic womanhood. But that a woman had to be a prostitute before she could realize her human potential is the worst condemnation of the Athenian family.

Such, says Engels, is the original form of the monogamous marriage as far as we can trace it back among the most civilized people of antiquity. It is not in any way the product of individual sex-love. It is on the contrary the first form of the family to be based on economic considerations following the victory of private property over primitive natural communal property. Its sole aim is to make the man supreme so as to propagate legitimate heirs. It is not the reconciliation of man and woman, let alone the highest form of such reconciliation. It enters history as the subjugation of one sex to the other. It announces a struggle between the sexes which is unknown throughout the whole prehistoric period. The first class opposition and oppression in history coincides with the antagonism of man and woman in monogamous marriage. Nevertheless it is a great historical step forward. Together with slavery and private wealth it begins the period of history, which has lasted until the contemporary world, in which the prosperity and development of some is achieved through the misery and frustration of others. It is the cellular form of civilized society, and in it one can see the nature of the oppositions and contradictions which pervade the whole.[28]

Monogamous marriage produces two contradictions. Firstly, prostitution, which is a remnant of group marriage and a rejection of monogamy for the man. Secondly, at the side of the husband who finds his sexual satisfaction elsewhere is the neglected wife who seeks a lover. Adultery becomes an unavoidable social institution. Thus we see in miniature the same class oppositions and contradictions as are to be found in the larger class-society.

Monogamous marriage does not by any means appear always in the harsh form it had in Ancient Greece. The greatest progress in the development of individual marriage comes with the entry of the Germans into history at the breakdown of the Roman Empire and with the emergence of individual sex-love hitherto unknown in the entire world. This advance is the result of the backward state of the Germans' social organization when they came in contact with Roman civilization. They are still living in pairing families and consequently take over into the monogamous system adopted from the Romans the position of women appropriate to the former family type. Even then individual sex-love does not develop exclusively or even chiefly as the love of husband and wife. The first historical form of sex-love was the chivalrous love of the Middle Ages which was by no means conjugal. In its classic form among the Provençals it led straight to adultery.

In the modern bourgeois form of monogamous marriage, at least in Protestant countries, the mutual love of the partners is supposed to be its basis. Yet this ideal, in Engels's view, hypocritically covers up a reality which remains conditioned by the class position of the partners, and marriage is to that extent always a matter of convenience. Marriage is also in effect the crassest prostitution for the woman, who only differs from the ordinary courtesan in that she does not let out her body on piece-work, but sells it once and for all into slavery. Sex-love in a relationship with a woman becomes, and can become, the real rule only among the oppressed classes. For here all the foundations of typical monogamy are cleared away: there is no property and hence no incentive to make male supremacy effective. Furthermore large-scale industry has removed the wife from the home, placed her in the factory and made her often the breadwinner of the family, thus effectively destroying the last basis on which male supremacy in the proletarian household can be built. The proletarian family is not strictly speaking monogamous any more. The eternal attendants of monogamy, prostitution and adultery, play only a vanishing part, and the wife has regained the right to dissolve the marriage.

In the modern bourgeois marriage there develops the idea of the legal equality of the partners. It is supposed to be a free contract, and in it both partners are to enjoy equal rights and duties. Hence it is claimed that women are not oppressed or subordinated to men, for the relation is one between equals. But, Engels argues, the position of women in bourgeois marriage is similar to that of the proletariat in the bourgeois socio-economic system. Formally speaking the proletariat has the same rights and duties as the bourgeois. The wage-relation is supposed to be a free contract between equal persons, but it is obvious that the real inequality of power between worker and capitalist ensures that the worker is forced to sell his labour in order to live, and has to accept a contract in which his surplus product, over and above his subsistence costs which he gets in wages, is appropriated by the capitalist. Similarly the equality of the contracting partners in marriage is formal only. They are limited in their choice in the first place by the interests of property, but more important the formal equality masks a real inequality of power. The older inequality of rights was not the cause of women's oppression, but its effect, which the declaration of a formal equality will not remove.

In the old communistic household the task entrusted to women of managing the household was as much a public, socially necessary industry as the procuring of the food supply by the men. With the patriarchal family and still more with the monogamous family, household management lost its public character. It no longer concerned society, but became a private service. The wife became the head-servant and was excluded from all participation in social production. Not until the coming of large-scale industry was the road to social production opened to women again, and then only to the proletarian wife. Even in her case she has to choose between carrying out her duties properly in the private service of her family, and taking part in public production. Thus the modern individual family is founded on the open or concealed domestic slavery of the wife. From the point of view of society, families are its basic molecules and are represented in the person of the husband, so that the wife is subsumed as a function within the family. The family in society has an individual existence and identity in which the personality and activity of the woman is lost.

In the great majority of cases in modern marriage it is the husband who earns the living and supports the family, and it is this fact which gives him a position of supremacy in the household, as Thompson also noted, without any need for the enjoyment of special rights or privileges. Within the family the man is the bourgeois and the wife is the proletarian. As in the economic world, where the real basis of the worker's oppression is laid bare only when complete legal equality is established, so also within the family. The peculiar character of the supremacy of the husband over the wife and the necessity for its overthrow by the creation of real social equality between them can be seen clearly only when the partners enjoy complete legal equality of rights. Then it will be plain that the first condition for the liberation of the wife is to bring the whole female sex back into public industry, and this requires that the monogamous family as the basic economic unit of society be abolished. With the disappearance of the private function of the wife and with her appearance in her own right in public society, this requirement will have been satisfied.[29]

According to Engels his contemporary society was approaching a social revolution in which the economic foundations of monogamy would be swept away. As we have seen, in Engels's view monogamy arose from the concentration of wealth in the hands of individual men, and from their desire to bequeath their wealth to their natural heirs. For this purpose the monogamy of the woman was required, but not that of the man. The coming socialist revolution, however, by transforming permanent heritable wealth, or the means of production, into social property will reduce to a minimum this concern for bequeathing and inheriting. Having arisen from economic causes, monogamy will disappear when those causes disappear.

With the transfer of the means of production into common ownership the single family ceases to be the basic economic unit of society. Private housekeeping is transformed into a social industry. The care and education of children becomes a public affair. This will not lead to a universal brothel; it is the family, not marriage which will disappear. The potentiality for individual sex-love will be fully realized unconstrained by considerations of class and property, and unhampered by responsibility for the care of children. By individual sex-love Engels does not mean simple sexual desire, but a reciprocal love in which a relationship of complete equality is the ideal. It has a degree of intensity and duration which makes lovers place mutual possession above everything else. It constitutes a new moral standard for the sexual relation. The bourgeois world proclaimed the love marriage as a human right, but in fact bourgeois class interests continued to restrict the freedom of marriage. Full freedom of marriage will be established only with the abolition of capitalist production, for then no motive for marriage will be left but mutual inclination. Since sexual love is by its nature exclusive, marriage based on it will continue to be individual marriage. But the supremacy of the man will disappear, and so also will the indissolubility of marriage, a product only of the interests of private property. Under socialism there will be full freedom of divorce. These, Engels admits, are largely negative considerations. The positive forms of sexual and social life that will take shape under socialism will be the creation of the new generation. They will make their own practices.[30]

August Bebel (1840–1913)

Bebel's book *Woman under Socialism* was first published in 1879 and hence before Engels's *Origin*, but it ran to an enormous number of editions and revisions (the presently available English edition being the 1904 translation from the 33rd German edition), and since it expresses in popular form the ideas of Marx and Engels it is sensible to treat it as an appendix to their work.

Bebel was one of the founders and leaders of the German Social Democratic Party, which claimed to be a Marxist party although its revolutionary nature and spirit has always been much doubted. His book takes the form, very similar to Engels's work, of an historical survey and analysis of the position of woman in the past – including the pre-historic past – and in the present, and ends with a sketch of the future under socialism. The conception of historical development is a Marxist materialist one. The question Bebel raises at the beginning of the work is how woman may unfold her powers so that she may become a complete and useful member of human society, enjoying equal rights with man. He sees this question as part of the general social question of what shape society must take so that no one is in want or exploited. But at the same time he holds that it is necessary to treat the woman question separately because of the extreme ignorance of woman's past and present, and because of the extremely inadequate notion of her calling. In this respect, he argues, the bourgeois individualist conception of woman's liberation, namely equal legal or formal rights within existing society, is unsatisfactory. The removal of all real dependence of women on men is required, and this calls for the abolition of wage and sexual slavery together. There can be no emancipation of humanity without the social independence and equality of the sexes.[31]

In his account of woman in the past Bebel closely follows the ideas of Morgan and Engels, especially with regard to the early periods, and nothing need be added to what has already been said above on this subject. In respect of his account of woman in the present he also follows Engels in holding up as an ideal the conception of marriage in bourgeois society, as a free spiritual and sexual union of man and woman founded only in the reciprocal love of the partners. Without this foundation marriage is held to be immoral. But the reality of bourgeois marriage is that property relations remain of fundamental importance to it. The marriage union should be arrived at uninfluenced by anything outside the spiritual and physical affinity of the partners. Since this is not the case in bourgeois society, the ideal cannot be realized in it. For most women modern marriage is a means of support which they must seek at any price, while men also enter marriage with wealth in mind. In every class and situation marriages and births are controlled by economic conditions.

In common with feminists of every type Bebel notes that the character of woman is formed by her training for domestic life. Those female characteristics that are widely and justly censured are the result not of woman's nature but of her training and conditions of life. A being irrationally brought up cannot bring others up rationally. The root cause of woman's vices lies in the fact that for man woman is first of all an object of enjoyment. Economically and socially she is unfree, and as a result she is bound to see in marriage her means of support. She depends on man and becomes a piece of property to him.

Bebel thinks that modern marriage is in the process of dissolution, a view he supports by reference to the rapid rise of the divorce rate in all European countries. He does not believe that there is any way of changing the unnatural conditions of marriage within capitalist society since for both partners in it private property is fundamental. Another social order is required to enable the marriage ideal to be realized.

Numerous women recognize the unsatisfactoriness of their position in existing society and demand economic self-support and independence, the freedom to engage in all pursuits for which their powers qualify them. Already women are increasingly torn from family life by industrial work. Marriage and the family in the bourgeois sense are being undermined, and it is thus senseless to hold up to women the ideal of a domestic life. This is especially true for the working class. The extension of female labour, however, should be seen as progress. It must be carried further. At present there exists a prejudice against women workers. The aim should be to establish a social condition in which full equality of all without distinction of sex should be the norm of conduct. This will be possible once the means of production are collectively owned. Then each works for society and in return is guaranteed what is necessary for the development of his faculties and for the enjoyment of life. Woman will be a full and useful member of this work force, a free being and free of man.

The whole trend of society, Bebel continues, is leading woman out of the narrow sphere of strictly domestic life to a full participation in the public life of the people. Once she is given the opportunity to develop her powers, woman will rise to a point of perfection in her being of which we can now have no adequate conception. Woman has the same right as man to the unfolding and free exercise of her faculties. She is human as well as he, and she should be free to dispose of herself as her own mistress. The only differences that can be justified are those established by nature. Men and women do differ physiologically and psychically, but these differences do not cancel their common humanity and the rights based thereon.[32]

Here Bebel is slipping into a manner of talking which derives from the individualist school and has its socialist form in pre- or non-Marxist theorists such as Thompson. The idea that individuals have rights of self-development in virtue of their humanity sets up individuals in the first place as the ground of moral worth in typical individualist fashion. The socialist reinterpretation of these individual rights involves first the claim that the rights must be real and not simply formal, and hence include a real equality of opportunity to develop one's faculties, and secondly the more strictly socialist idea that the development of these faculties will occur through cooperative production in which each works for society and not for himself. The difficulty in establishing the coherence of this combination has already been touched upon, a difficulty which Marx himself avoids by rejecting the language of individualism in the first place. In this respect, as in others, Bebel reveals an inadequate grasp of the thought he purports to adhere to.

Yet for both Marx and Bebel the objective is the same: under socialism each individual will be placed in a position to be able to develop his powers to his own advantage and to that of the collectivity at the same time, so that no conflict of interest between individual and collectivity can occur. The harmony of interests will be such that the thought of ruling and injuring others may not even be conceived by the individual.

It is the class state, Bebel argues, which upholds the present domination of one sex by the other, and hence woman has a natural alliance to make with the working class for the purposes of overthrowing that state. The evils of the capitalist system result from the lack of social control of production: these evils are overproduction, trade crises and slumps. They will become so evident to the feeling and sight of the vast majority that they will no longer be tolerable and will produce an irresistible desire for a radical change, which will sweep away the old society and bring in the new.

Once society takes control of the means of production, it will give equality of existence to all. But as to how this will be achieved and under what conditions, Bebel shows the usual Marxist modesty by leaving it to the future generation to determine. He limits himself to the general principles of the new society. These involve the duty to work of all able persons without distinction of sex. This is an organic law of socialized society. The work will be moderate, agreeable, varied and productive. It will afford to each the fullest possible measure of the amenities of life. Everyone will decide for himself the pursuit he wishes to follow, and the large number of different fields of activity will cater to the taste of all. A central administration will attend to the equalization of supply and demand for labour, and there will be a system of labour organized on a plan of absolute liberty and democratic equality in which each stands for all and all stand for each, and the sense of solidarity reigns supreme. In the new order the gratification of the ego and the promotion of the common weal harmonize. The law of human association under which the new order embarks on its journey is that each must develop himself fully according to his inclination and faculties, and thereby the whole will be served.[33]

All these principles apply to women as much as to men. An essential condition for their application to women is, however, women's liberation from household work. Private household work will be abolished and will become public work in the form of public kitchens, centralized heating, laundry and cleaning services. Yet Bebel appears to take for granted that women will still be doing this sort of work, only now they will be doing it as public servants paid for the job.

Woman in the future, then, will be an equal worker in a public realm, a socially and economically independent being. She will have had the same education as men, and will choose her occupation in accordance with her inclinations and abilities as men do, and will work under identical conditions with men. As a mother she will be supported by public services, by nurses and teachers and female friends, who will help her when in need. In love she will be unrestricted and free. She will choose and end her bond with a man solely according to her own inclinations, for the relation is a private one to be celebrated without the aid and control of a functionary. The satisfaction of the sexual instinct is a private concern of no interest to society, so long as there is no injury to others.[34]

Thus we see once again that the socialist solution to the woman question is to liberate woman from the private functions of wife and mother and make her into a public worker in a socialized economy. So far as is possible the traditional private functions of the woman are to become public ones, although still to be performed by women as public servants. Private mothering is to be reduced to a minimum through the development of nurseries which relieve the mother of the care of her children, and the private household becomes, much as in Fourier's phalanstery, a private room in a public hotel controlled by centralized services.

Like Engels, Bebel sees in the advantages of the new order the possibility of realizing to the full the bourgeois ideal of individual sex-love between a man and a woman. Unrestricted by the care of children, by considerations of money, or by the constraints of society, individuals will bind themselves to each other on the basis of pure reciprocal love alone. Engels and Bebel thus make a radical distinction between marriage and the family. It is not the marriage tie to a man that in itself subordinates the woman to a private function in a purely domestic life. It is the monogamous family to which the woman is subject. The typical socialist solution of abolishing the family is not intended by the socialist theorists whom I have been considering, with the possible exception of Fourier, to be the abolition of the marriage tie, understood as a private bond between a man and a woman based on love and expressed in a shared life.

Charlotte Perkins Gilman (1860–1935)

The above distinction between the institutions of marriage and of the family also plays an important part in the work of the non-Marxist socialist feminist Charlotte Perkins Gilman whose book *Women and Economics*, published in 1898 in America, was widely read and influential. Her socialist ideas were worked out within the general framework of a social Darwinist conception. Social Darwinism itself was a widely held view at the end of the nineteenth century, but its most fashionable expression was in the work of Herbert Spencer, who was not a socialist at all but an extreme type of individualist.[35] Social Darwinism was the application to the understanding of human society of Charles Darwin's conception of the nature and processes of the evolution of species. In general terms it consisted in the conception of man as the product of the interaction of heredity and environment. Strictly speaking one might think such a conception must deny the nature of man as a free being altogether, whether that freedom is understood in individualist or socialist terms. Yet neither Spencer nor Gilman in their opposite ways were much troubled by this combination of an overall determinism with human freedom.

Thus for Gilman the individual is seen as a creature of his environment, part of which is his social environment within which economic conditions are the most important element. In

these terms she develops her account of the causes of female subordination and of the particular nature of female character. She
notes first of all that the dependence in the human race of the
female on the male for her food is unparalleled in other species.
The entire female sex lives in a relation of economic dependence,
and hence for her the economic status is relative to the sex-
relation. Gilman includes in this generalization situations where
the female works to produce food, as for example the peasant
woman. In such cases, however, her labour is the property of a
man, so that despite being a producer she remains dependent.[36]

Gilman also considers the claim that women are not dependent on men for their livelihood because they contribute to a
common life as wives and mothers. But, she argues, wives who
do housework have no economic independence. To have economic independence is to be in the position of giving to others the
equivalent of what others give one. It is to pay for what one
acquires, and to obtain the wherewithal to pay through one's
own work. Such economic independence is not supposed to be
incompatible with the general interdependence of individuals in
society: the independence of individuals consists in their mutual
dependence and is distinguished from the absolute dependence
of the one on the other. Thus women do not get paid for maintaining a home or for acting as mothers, and hence whatever her
formal rights the female as wife and mother is economically
dependent.

Gilman asks whether this dependence is necessary. She does
not think that maternal duties are all-absorbing. It is home-
service, not child-service, that keeps the housewife on her feet all
day. If this time were used for economic production, women
could have an independent living within the institution of monogamous marriage. Gilman sees the monogamous marriage as the
result of a social development which is best calculated to advance
the interests of both individual and society. This development is
natural in the sense of according with the needs of the organism.
But it has been accompanied by an unnatural development which
ensures that we do not live at peace within the monogamous
union. This is the excessive development of the sex-distinction
which in turn produces excessive sex-attraction and sex-
indulgence. The excessive development of the sex-instinct itself

is the result of an evolutionary development following upon the female's economic dependence on the male.[37]

Gilman goes on to distinguish between the self-preservation of the individual and race-preservation. These are often opposed. A limit on the extent of the sex-distinction is necessary for race-preservation in a species. The force of natural selection, demanding and producing an identical race, acts as a check on the process of sexual selection which generates differences in the characteristics of the sexes. But when, as in the case of the human race in Gilman's view, sex-distinction becomes so excessive as to impede and pervert the progress of the race, it has become unnatural. The mechanism for explaining this unnatural development is simple. When the male became master of the female, the economic environment encouraged the growth of the sex-distinction, for the sex-distinction was now the woman's way of getting a livelihood. Hence woman is modified to sex to an excessive degree. As Gilman among others notes, woman was generally referred to as 'the sex'.

Gilman, like most nineteenth-century feminists, accepts that there are inherited sex-linked behaviour characteristics: belligerence and dominance in the male, modesty and timidity in the female. With these she is not concerned, but rather with the manifestation of the sex-distinction in the production of excessive sex-energy. The male directs this excess energy partly into work activity in industry, art and so on. He sublimates it. But in doing so he transforms the sexual energy into a non-sexual human activity. Women, on the other hand, do not have a sphere of work in which their sex-energies can be given a human expression, and so remain directly over-sexed. This produces unfavourable results for the woman, her husband and children, and for the race. It manifests itself in the search for self-realization through a life dedicated to the love-passion, which cannot be satisfied within the monogamous union. Against this identification of woman with her sexual nature Gilman reaffirms the fundamental feminist claim that woman is like man primarily a person, a human being.[38]

According to Gilman the origin of female dependence on the male consists in nothing more complicated than the enslavement of the one by the other. The consequent restriction of woman's labour to the home has prevented her from participating in the great development of human work through specialization and organization whereby the organic life of society has evolved. Woman's labour remains technically at a primitive level compared with the achievements of the race as a whole. But this exclusion of the female from social progress is ending. The greatest and most beneficial changes of the nineteenth century have been the beginning of women's involvement in the life of society.

The inevitable trend of human society is towards a higher civilization. But while the participation in this trend is confined to one sex, it increases the distinction between the sexes, and thereby weakens the nation and ensures its eventual fall. A civilized state is one in which its members live in an organic industrial relationship. In it each can live only by serving others; each has to develop special functions of value to society but of no direct use to the individual, and hence attains his self-realization only through dependence on the whole. This organic civilization is the glory of the human race from which woman has been excluded. As a result only man is human, and woman is stunted in her human growth.

The basic condition of present human life is this organic social relation, the interchange of functional service. Wealth is a social product. Society is an organization composed of individuals living in organic relation. The specialization of labour and the exchange of its products in a social body is identical in its nature with the specialization and exchange of function in the natural individual body. It involves the gradual subordination of individual effort to collective effort for the collective good, not out of altruism but out of economic necessity. Yet against the trend towards this collective civilization society retains within itself rudimentary impulses surviving from an earlier condition, namely individualist self-seeking without regard to others. The consequent lack of adjustment between individual and social interest is the cause of the contemporary economic troubles. Behind this individualism lies the individualist nature of the sexuo-economic relation. The sex-relation is unavoidably individual and not social. But the combination of the sex-relation with the economic relation in the monogamous union ensures the preservation of individualist attitudes within an increasingly collec-tivist society. The individual in his economic relations is made selfish by his family interests. Yet the sinking of personal interests in common interests is what the evolving spirit of socialism requires.[39]

Gilman does not mean that the spirit of socialism is incompatible with the monogamous sex-union: quite the contrary provided both parties to the union are independent. But by making the woman dependent on the marriage union we are preserving her in a position of primitive individual competition, and the social spirit is not developed in her. Also the sex-interest of the man in this situation drives him to the pursuit of individual economic gain in order to get and maintain a wife. But for himself and by himself the individual would work for society, and once we see that the pure lasting monogamous union does not require the economic dependence of the woman, and that the pair are free to combine with others in economic relations, the tendency to think of the spirit of socialism and devotion to humanity as incompatible with our natural inclinations will disappear. Work for its own sake is the natural expression of human energy, and the distinguishing characteristic of humanity. Once again women are denied participation in this creative impulse of humanity by their position of economic dependence.

In accordance with her evolutionary conception Gilman holds that the sexuo-economic relation was at one time advantageous to society, but that with the development of organic interdependence this is no longer so. The woman's movement is an expression of this fact, and of the inevitability of the changes that are occurring. It is only necessary to make these ideas clear in our minds, for us to withdraw the futile opposition of our wills to it.

Social cooperation requires the development of a common consciousness. The first steps in this development were taken in the formation of the mother/child relation, and subsequently through the inclusion of the male in the common life of the family. In this way the individualist male began to learn to work for others. To do this he had to acquire the conserving instincts of the female. Gilman holds that from the point of view of social development the female was initially the superior sex because of her capacity to coordinate. In her view, indeed, the female constitutes the mainstream of the life of the race. The development of the male to full racial equality with the female, however, required the female's temporary subjection in order that her superiority should not prevent the necessary development of humanity through the creation of an organic social world under the force of male energy. But that necessary subjection of the female has involved the suppression of the vast storage battery of female energy.

The time has come in which this suppression is no longer necessary. We know that it is time to change because we are already changing. The main advance is towards economic equality and freedom for both men and women. The full development of democracy requires individual liberty, and the possession of this by women will permit the completion of collective industry. At the same time the higher development of social life will make higher monogamous unions possible.

Woman and her image are changing. She is, and is represented in art as, more active with ideas and purposes of her own. She has become and is becoming more individualized. Once again it is the development of economic specialization which is bringing about this result by drawing woman out of the home into social industry, and thereby breaking up that relic of the patriarchal age – the family as an economic unit. Women's work has become a specialized function in the public world, and women have left home to follow it. Woman's differentiation and individualization is the result of being formed in this public world, and as a consequence the more primitive, undifferentiated conditions of life and work in the family are intolerable to her. Housework in particular with its constant changes is dissatisfying to the differentiated and specialized modern brain.

Gilman's criticism of the family is directed at its existence as an economic and social unit, as a place of work for woman and as a social whole with its own interest. But the family in this sense is not essential to woman's true role as wife and mother. The traditional woman's place in the family is justified on the grounds that it provides the benefit of a specialized motherhood. But Gilman rejects this claim. Motherhood, like anything else, must be judged by its service to the human race. It comprises an educative and reproductive function. The former, she argues, is now a racial and not an individual function, and mothers are very deficient in their fulfilment of it. They receive no training, and have only the great maternal love without informed intelligence to guide it. As for the reproductive function, it is performed worse in the human species than in any animal species, and this is because woman is so specialized on it. The more freely a woman engages in natural human industry, in Gilman's view, the more adequately does she fulfil the reproductive function.

Gilman also rejects out of hand the idea that woman provides for the improvement of the race through the maintenance of the sanctuary of the home. The traditional home does indeed need a fulltime woman to maintain it, but for Gilman the traditional home must go. Certain functions such as private feeding and the private rearing of children must go. Gilman distinguishes in a way similar to Engels and Bebel between marriage and the family. The family is a social whole, a little state. For Gilman it is a gradually disappearing survival of the original undifferentiated tribal horde. Monogamous marriage on the other hand represents the increasing development of high social life. It improves and strengthens in direct relation to the decline of the family. For the family requires the economic dependence of the woman, while the conditions of the highest marriage relation are those of economic independence and equality of the partners.[40]

The traditional family is fed, cleaned and generally cared for in the home by amateurs. These functions would be performed better by experts. So like Fourier, Gilman wants us to live in apartment houses with common kitchens, communal dining and centralized and professional cleaning services. Nurseries and kindergarten staffed by trained persons would be provided. The apartment would contain private rooms, and the children of the married couple would continue to live with them. But there would be as little common family life as possible. The home with its individual rooms would become the personal expression of its occupants.

Gilman believes that this residual family home is still necessary for the development of children. Women will retain some degree of maternal function and will choose professions compatible with it. But it will be a greatly reduced function. We need, Gilman thinks, a radical change in the method of child culture.

Individuation and specialization have progressed to such an extent that the psychic conditions of the traditional communal home life are no longer tolerable. Children are increasingly restless. The conditions in which they are now reared are not suitable for the cultivation in them of the qualities needed in socialized man — those of honour, duty to work and devotion to the social good. On the contrary the children see only the devotion of their parents to themselves. This produces an excessive demand for personal attention and an excessive self-consciousness. Were a baby to spend several hours a day among other babies, it would acquire a different opinion of itself: it would learn that it was only one among many.

Gilman observes that the care and training of little children is becoming an object of increasing attention and expertise. Mothers should not be expected to provide these services. Education is a collective human function and requires professional training. This is not to say that the mother/child relation is to be abolished, but rather supplemented. The child still needs the personal touch which that relation provides. But the relation has become too intensely personal with the result that the child thinks too much of itself. Being together with others it will learn that the 'we' constitutes humanity. Hence the conditions which will liberate woman for the full development of her humanity in the public world are also those which will provide a better environment for the moral and social growth of the child.

It must be admitted that Gilman in her criticisms of the family reveals an uncertainty as to whether its unsatisfactory nature vis à vis its members consists in its communal life which suppresses their individuality or in the production in them of an excessive personal concern and insufficient communal spirit. If what is wrong with the family is that it does not allow sufficiently for the individuality of its members because it insists on communal forms, meals and living rooms, then why is the communal life of the nursery and kindergarten supposed to be so good for the child? On the other hand, if the self-consciousness of individuality, which Gilman everywhere celebrates, is given its most extreme development in the child through the personal relations and privacy of the family, how can it be sensible to wish to substitute a more communal and less individualized experience for it?

If Gilman's thought in this matter is uncertain, it is because she shows an awareness, not to be found in the other socialist feminists discussed in this chapter, that the modern family to some extent constitutes the conditions under which the individuality of the child is formed and flourishes. For the most part socialist theorists, including and perhaps especially Marx, treat the development of individuality is unproblematic. Human beings are naturally individuals, and the only problem is to ensure that this individuality is not perverted by private forms of life into egoism. Do away with these perverted forms, substitute cooperative practices, and the individuality of men and women will develop naturally. The abolition of the family and the collectivization of the nurture and education of children presents no problems. The underlying assumption in this attitude is that there is no conflict between the individual and society, but that the individual in his particular life expresses and realizes the life of the social whole. It is only when the individual becomes a member of a group smaller than society as a whole, such as the family, that a gap between his individual interest and the interest of society emerges. Gilman shares this conception when she argues that it is the family based on the sexuo-economic relations that preserves individualistic and competitive desires, and that the individual left to himself naturally seeks the social good. Yet her doubts regarding the conditions of the formation of individuality remain and are expressed in her unwillingness to see the family and its personal relations abolished altogether.

Alexandra Kollontai (1872–1952) and the Russian Revolution

Alexandra Kollontai was born into an aristocratic Russian family, but becoming interested in the conditions of factory workers, both male and female, was drawn into socialist circles and became an active member of the Russian Social Democratic Party – a Marxist party.[41] During World War I she joined the Bolshevik wing of the party and played an important role in the seizure of power by the Bolsheviks in October 1917. As a Marxist Kollontai's views on the woman question were formed by the writings of Engels and Bebel. From this perspective she saw the question of women's liberation as part of the general struggle for socialism against capitalism, and not as a separate issue opposing women to men more generally.[42] In respect of the basic Marxist conception of women's liberation Kollontai then had nothing new to contribute; she was a propagandist of existing ideas. However, she upheld more particularly in her life and writings the need for women to participate actively in the work of their own liberation through separate women's organizations within the party, and not to wait passively for the socialist revolution to hand them their liberation on a plate. Furthermore, she devoted herself to thinking through in greater detail the general idea of women's freedom in socialist society adumbrated by Engels and Bebel.

Kollontai became convinced of the need to organize women separately within the Social Democratic Party because of woman's special situation, as not only a worker but a mother also, and therefore with needs not catered for by the general workers' struggle.[43] Her early attempts to secure separate organization were met with some hostility by male members of the party, but Kollontai was successful in her aims, and after the Bolshevik seizure of power obtained further institutional recognition of women's special position. In the early days of the revolution Kollontai was appointed Commissar of Social Welfare, and later became head of the Central Women's Department. She was responsible for drafting the new laws on women's status and on marriage which aimed to implement the Marxist conception of women's freedom and equality.

This conception, it will be recalled, involved the abolition of the family and private household on the one hand, and the full integration of women in the public work force on the other. These, together with the question of a new sexual morality for communist society, are the central themes of Kollontai's writing. The basic idea to be found in her work at different periods of her career is that society will take responsibility for the needs of the mother and for the care of young children. There will be special maternity homes where the woman gives birth and nurses her infant. When the mother becomes strong enough she returns to her normal work and the child is cared for in special homes run by experienced nurses. The mother will be free to visit the child as she wishes, so that only the joyful aspects of maternity are supposed to remain.[44] Meanwhile the other aspect of woman's task in the family – household work – is integrated into the national economy through the creation of public kitchens and restaurants, and central cleaning and laundry services.

With the establishment of the Communist State and its drive to organize the whole of society from the centre, the collectivist element in the Marxist ideas of Kollontai becomes more explicit. The organizational objectives remain the same – the destruction of the private family and household – but the rhetoric puts particular emphasis on the need to subordinate the individual to the claims of the collective. The emancipation of women from the burden of maternity is said to take place through the care of the young becoming a social state concern. Maternity is a social task carried out by women to satisfy society's interest in a continued flow of healthy members. The mother no longer belongs to herself but to the collective. Her first obligation to it is to give birth and secondly to breastfeed her baby. Thereafter the mother is not necessary for the child. Kollontai admits the existence of a strong maternal instinct, but believes that it is not an exclusive one and that it can be extended by the women nurses to all the children in their care. Having performed her maternal duty to the collective the mother is free to take her place in the labour force again. This, Kollontai says, is the key to the solution of the complex question of maternity; that women be viewed as essentially a labour unit, so that maternity constitutes only a brief interruption in the exercise of their true function.[45]

These ideas, reiterated in the later work *Communism and the Family*, cannot be said to add anything but detail to the general conceptions of women's liberation under socialism. Kollontai, however, also wrote on the problems of sexual love under the new order, and her ideas here do not follow those of her predecessors quite so closely. Engels and Bebel believed that, with the disappearance of the compulsion and inequality of bourgeois marriage, the bourgeois ideal of a lasting love-union between the free and equal men and women of socialist society would be fully realized. Such unions would be based on mutual agreement and would be ended on the same basis. Love affairs would not be the concern of society, and it would be up to individuals to regulate them in accordance with their own wishes, but it was expected that the regulation would be conducted in terms of the love-ideal.

Kollontai adopts much of this conception, but places it in a somewhat different perspective. For although she says that, once relations between the sexes cease to perform the economic and social functions of the former family, they are no longer the concern of the collective, she nevertheless poses the question of the morality of sexual relations under socialism in this form: 'What kind of relations between the sexes would be in the best interests of the workers' collective?' Her answer is that relations should be governed by two criteria: firstly, the health of the working population, and secondly the development of inner bonds of solidarity within the collective. With regard to the former she holds the view that the satisfaction of sexual desire should be considered as natural as the satisfaction of other needs such as hunger and thirst. Satisfaction of healthy and natural instincts ceases to be normal only when the boundaries of hygiene are overstepped. But the health interests of the collective as well as those of the individual are involved. Communist morality in her view condemns unhealthy and unnatural sex. But it also criticizes sexual restraint. Frequent changes of sexual partner she does not consider to be necessarily unhealthy. Sex, based on physical attraction alone and not attended by love or fleeting passion, she does not approve of and calls wingless Eros, to be contrasted with winged Eros which is sex plus emotion.[46] These views of Kollontai's on sex came under attack from the communist authorities, including Lenin himself. They were characterized as the glass of water notion of sex, the notion that the sex act should be seen as equivalent to the drinking of a glass of water. Clearly this is a considerable distortion of Kollontai's ideas.[47]

Nevertheless, it is the case that Kollontai finds acceptable a greater degree of sexual promiscuity, provided that it is accompanied by emotion or passion, than appears to be envisaged by her Victorian predecessors. A major reason for this complaisance is her belief that the isolation of the loving couple as a special unit is bad for the collective. The needs and interests of the individual must be subordinate to the interests and aims of the collective. Sexual love, as only one aspect of life, must not be allowed to overshadow other facets of the relation of the individual to the collective. Communist morality demands that the young be educated so that the personality of the individual be developed to the full, but, Kollontai argues, this requires the development of many and varied bonds of love and friendship between people. The old ideal was that everything should be done for the sake of the loved one. Communist morality demands that everything should be done for the sake of the collective. Thus the less exclusive sexual love is and the more it is spread around, the closer will the emotional ties of all members of the collective be to each other.

It is the possessive aspect of exclusive sexual love that Kollontai finds so undesirable. Such possessiveness is the product of capitalist socio-economic relations based on private property, and of the individualistic psyche fostered by the bourgeois ideology. The latter produces an unavoidable loneliness of spirit which the individual seeks to escape by finding a sexual soulmate. The consequence is an unhealthy and predatory desire to cling to and possess the loved one, which prevents us following the simplest rule of love, that the other should be treated with great consideration.

The new sexual relations emerging in communist society based on the complete freedom and equality of the lovers will, in Kollontai's view, be incompatible with this jealous and proprietary attitude. They will involve the radical reform of the human psyche and, being based on the comradeship of independent workers, will not permit of either partner belonging to the other. A person may need more than one love-relation. Indeed, the interest of the working class is in a wider range of relations which make the collective stronger. The aim of proletarian morality, in her view, is that the qualities of love-comradeship should be displayed in relations with all members of the collective. In the future communist society the exclusiveness and separation of the loving pair will become psychologically inconceivable.[48]

In 1921 Kollontai lent her support and advocacy to the Workers' Opposition movement which criticized the ruling communist party for substituting itself for the self-management of the workers. This movement was defeated and suppressed and Kollontai had to resign from her post as head of the Central Women's Department. Subsequently, she received diplomatic appointments abroad and played no further part in the development of

Soviet policy towards women. In fact the Soviet Government proceeded to reverse the revolution's plans for liberating women, and came to endorse and support the private family and women's maternal role in it, attacking at the same time the conception of communist sexual ethics propagated by Kollontai.

In the early days of the revolution, among the measures enacted with a view to liberating women, were the transformation of marriage into simple civil registration with complete equality of rights and divorce by mutual agreement; abortion on demand; plans for development of collectivized child care and centralized household services. However, such plans were largely unfulfilled. The government was too poor and too beset by the immediate demands of survival to give much money or attention to this problem. Furthermore, the liberal marriage, divorce and abortion laws, together with large-scale unemployment for women, led to a serious deterioration in women's security. In the 1920s official government policy was reversed and the aim became to rehabilitate and preserve the family. Abortion was made illegal, divorce more difficult, and promiscuous sexuality morally unacceptable. This return to the values of the family did not, however, involve an abolition of the legal equality of men and women in marriage, or the discouragement of women from seeking careers outside the home, or the complete abandonment of welfare services for the working mother. It has meant rather that the woman works outside the home as well as fulfilling the traditional woman's roles in it.[49]

This betrayal of the original socialist idea of women's freedom is often attributed to the particular difficulties and deficiencies of Soviet socialism. The new state, impoverished by a crippling civil war, generally held back by the primitiveness of the Russian economy, could not provide in sufficient quantity and quality the collective services that were to be the substitute for women's private household and maternal tasks. However, such explanations do not satisfy many contemporary socialist feminists influenced by the radical movement of the 1960s and 1970s. These theorists, to be discussed in the next chapter, are inclined to attribute the failure of socialist societies to realize the feminist ideal to an inadequate theoretical analysis and understanding of woman's roles in the family.

3 Radical Feminism

Introduction

In this chapter my main concern will be to bring out what is distinctive in the feminist thought of the period after World War II and particularly of the period of the 1960s and 1970s in which feminist thought and organization were given new life and new directions. Those who call themselves radical feminists primarily represent this development in feminism, and it is on their thought that I shall concentrate. There continue to be, of course, individualist and socialist feminists of an apparently more classic variety. But these latter tend to be affected by the radical feminist challenge, and attempt to incorporate the fundamental idea of radical feminism into their own positions. These positions are thereby transformed.

The main difference between the new doctrine of radical feminism and the older views centres on their respective conceptions of the nature of women. While the classic individualist and socialist feminists are in agreement with contemporary feminists in holding that woman's fundamental nature is, like that of man's, to be a free, self-forming being, which is indeed on my view the central feminist idea, at the same time they accept that woman, like man, has a sexual nature, expressed in specifically feminine traits and behaviour. For the nineteenth-century individualist this feminine nature justifies woman's continued existence in the family as wife and mother. In the case of the socialists the belief in such a nature is implied in their assumption that the transformation of traditional women's jobs from the private into the public sphere will not affect their sexual character. In complete contrast, the radical feminist denies that there is any such sexual nature of human beings. Sexually differentiated behaviour patterns are in their view wholly attributable to the different social formations of men and women, the function of which is essentially to support the institution of male dominance.

97

or patriarchy. As a consequence, a more radical and deep-rooted antagonism between men and women comes to the fore in their thought.

Some care, however, must be taken in presenting this distinction. The classic feminists are aware of the way in which woman's feminine character is given specific and unnatural forms by male-dominated society. They desire to see a change in the education of women, and in the values and style of life on the basis of which women are formed. Yet they do not thereby deny that women have a sexual nature. Indeed, in the case of Fuller this nature is positively affirmed in ways which would do justice to the conceptions of a traditional anti-feminist. But Fuller sees no conflict between the primacy of woman's free personality and her possession of a sexual nature. Thus the difference between the nineteenth-century and contemporary radical feminists amounts to this: that the former accept a limited sexual nature as justifying appropriate roles in what is a fundamentally free human life, while the latter deny any sexual nature and demand the abolition of all sexually differentiated roles in an androgynous world.

Although the focus of this chapter will be on radical feminism, I shall begin with an account of the work of Simone de Beauvoir, who wrote her important and influential book *The Second Sex* two decades before radical feminism made its appearance. Beauvoir accepts a limited form of the idea of woman's sexual nature, but the sharpening and deepening of the antagonism between men and women is evident in her work. In the works of those feminists writing at the end of the 1960s, such as Eva Figes and Germaine Greer who are not themselves identified with radical feminism, even Beauvoir's limited conception of woman's sexual nature disappears. An account of their ideas and of those of the Freudian Marxists, Charles Reich and Herbert Marcuse, who were important influences on the formation of the thought of the New Left movement from which radical feminism sprang, will precede the discussion of radical feminism itself.

Simone de Beauvoir (b. 1908)

Beauvoir tells us that her book is not so much concerned with claiming any rights for women as with understanding woman's nature and her position in the world.[1] This is misleading in so far as it implies that no conclusions are drawn from the analysis as to woman's appropriate place in society. It is true that the overwhelming part of a large work is devoted to various forms of analysis, but the direction in which the analysis points cannot be mistaken. At the same time it is in the depth of the analysis and the far-reaching exploration of the forms and extent of woman's subordination to man, and of the impediments to her full freedom as an active human being, that Beauvoir's work is so important for subsequent feminist thought.

She begins with the question: 'What is woman?' She denies that woman can be understood either in terms of her biological function or in terms of the idea of the eternal feminine, that is to say of woman's essentially feminine nature. This latter conception is the traditional one, she admits. It involves seeing woman as defined by her sex, and hence defined relatively to man. This is to be contrasted with the traditional definition of man. Man is not essentially masculine, but a free or autonomous being. He is thus defined independently of his relation to woman. The result is the imbalance and inequality between man and woman.

Beauvoir, in her rejection of this traditional conception, expresses once again the essential feminist idea that woman has the same nature as man, and is like him a free and creative being. Each should be defined independently of the other, and being of equal worth should have equal rights. The individualist's formally equal rights, however, are necessary but not sufficient. Beauvoir accepts the socialist critique of such rights, but her account of woman's subjection is very far from being a socialist one. It is rather an existentialist one derived from the thought of Jean-Paul Sartre. The essentially free individual, in seeking to realize his freedom, comes up against the consciousness of other human beings. He has an existence in their consciousness, and as such is an object for them, a being with a determinate character rather than a free subject. To that extent the other imposes an identity on the individual and denies his character as a free subject. As a free subject he and he alone determines what he is. At the same time he maintains his independence of that determinate character by never identifying himself wholly with it, but always goes beyond it by seeking some future condition. There appears to be, then, an inherent antagonism between each free subject. Each sees the other as a threat to his freedom, and in order to overcome this he attempts to subordinate the other, to deny the other's freedom, and make the other exist solely as a particular determinate being relative to him. Beauvoir's work is the application of this idea to the understanding of woman in her relations with man.

In some distant past men as a whole faced women as a whole in the struggle to assert their freedom. This battle was resolved in favour of the men, and women, failing to assert their autonomy, were defined in terms of their existence for men. This historical defeat of women is one in which each new generation of women acquiesces by failing to affirm its freedom. Because women have never overcome this defeat, it appears an unavoidable necessity beyond possibility of change. But Beauvoir denies that the nature of woman is given. As inherently free subject woman is to define her own content. Even the women's movement of the nineteenth and twentieth centuries does not appear to Beauvoir as an exercise of freedom. Their efforts for change have been only a symbolic agitation, she believes. Women have gained only what men have been willing to grant. They have *taken* nothing, but have been content to receive, and hence have remained passive recipients defined by men. The reason for this lies in women's lack of the concrete means of organizing themselves in a unit which could stand face to face with a correlative unit. They have no past, no history, no religion of their own, no solidarity. They live dispersed among males. Their solidarity is with the interests of their husbands. Here is the basic trait of woman as defined by man, according to Beauvoir. She is the dependent other in a totality of which the two components are necessary to one another.[2]

Thus Beauvoir's book is implicitly a call to woman to assert her autonomy in defining herself against man. The goal is not so much to claim what man has, his rights, nor to participate with men in a common socialist liberation, but to win her existence as free subject by defining her own identity, giving herself a past and creating for herself a solidarity with other women. This does not imply, according to Beauvoir, that unity with man is impossible, any more than in her view the basic existentialist idea precludes unity between men. But this unity is always problematic.

It requires a recognition of reciprocity, a *mitsein* or being together. But here Beauvoir skates over the inherent difficulty in the Sartrean existentialist project for a common freedom. Since the free subject defines himself as free over and against the other, the *mitsein* with the other requires their mutual opposition to a third. This is no true unity but a temporary alliance of some against the freedom of others.

The claim that woman suffered an historical defeat in a struggle with man for freedom is not to be understood literally. In Beauvoir's view, man developed his freedom over and against woman by treating her as the other and subjecting her. Woman failed to develop her subjectivity, not because she literally fought and lost, but for reasons of a biological and historical nature. But an inherently free being, the existentialist argues, is responsible for its failure to develop that freedom, and hence woman is responsible for her own subjection. It is her own project to be the other for man. To become free, she must alter her project.

The first part of Beauvoir's work is devoted to a critique of major conceptions of woman's subordination which leave, in her view, no room for woman's freedom. Biology, for Beauvoir, does not determine woman's nature, but it powerfully affects and in part explains her history. The fundamental difference between male and female in mammalian species is that after coition the male is free to resume his individuality or separateness, while the female has new life attached to her. The female renounces her separateness for the benefit of the species. She maintains life, while the male creates. In this way the individuality of the female is opposed by the interests of the species. Woman as the most individualized of female mammals feels this conflict most sharply. In no other female is the enslavement of the organism to reproduction more demanding or, physically, more unwillingly accepted. Man is much more favoured by biology. His sex life is not in opposition to his existence as a person.

These biological considerations are extremely important but they do not inexorably determine woman's destiny in Beauvoir's view. The bearing of maternity on individual life is governed by social conditions, by the number of births required of women, by the degree of hygienic care, by the existence of contraception. Woman is thus not this biological destiny, but what humanity has made of the biological female in the course of its history.[3]

Beauvoir, in common with many subsequent feminists, sees in Freudian psychoanalytic theory an alternative account of woman's destiny and subordination, which has to be combated if her freedom is to be affirmed. Beauvoir sees that for Freud also it is not nature that defines woman as a subordinate and dependent being, but woman herself in her own emotional development. But the Freudian theory still involves the denial of freedom. It rejects the idea of the self-defining choice, and substitutes in its place emotional compulsions and prohibitions deriving from the girl's attitudes to her own body in the social situation of the family. Beauvoir does not deny the force of the Freudian explanation, but she does deny that woman must respond to her situation in the way described in Freudian theory. Woman, as free being, can succeed in establishing her subjectivity, and hence in rejecting the project whereby she exists primarily as a sexual object for man.[4]

Beauvoir also attacks the Marxist explanation of woman's oppression. It is, like the biological and Freudian explanations, a partial one only. Private property cannot in itself explain woman's oppression. It is true that woman's incapacity for labour as a result of her preoccupation with the home brought her ruin in a context in which man's desire for transcendence led him to projects of expansion and wealth. But underlying this transformation is the imperialism of the human consciousness seeking to exercise sovereignty by imposing itself on the external world. If human consciousness did not include the other as something calling forth the aspiration to dominate, the invention of new productive forces would not have caused the oppression of women.

Furthermore woman cannot simply be regarded as a worker, and cannot be liberated simply by becoming a specialized worker. For her reproductive function is as important as her productive function. Hence merely to say that a socialist economy will abolish the family is an abstract solution. It is impossible to treat maternity as a task or service, which can be seen as part of socialized labour. In maternity, Beauvoir claims, essential values are involved for the woman. By this she means that maternity is woman's physiological destiny or natural calling. It cannot be transformed into a purely social function, although it can be subject to human control and be made compatible with woman's freedom.[5]

Having rejected these major structural explanations of woman's subordination on the grounds that they contain elements which have their explanatory force only within the more general existentialist conception of human subjectivity, Beauvoir proceeds to an existentialist interpretation of woman's history, of which we may consider some salient points.

She begins with nomadic life. The key to the whole mystery of woman's subordination lies in the fact that while man realizes himself in projects towards a different future through which he transcends his given existence and actualizes his freedom, woman is, through her biological destiny, directed towards the repetition of life. The domestic labours that fell to her lot, because they were compatible with the cares of maternity, imprisoned her in repetition and immanence. Man, on the other hand, has from the beginning of time been an inventor. He sets up goals and opens up the roads to them. He bursts out of the present towards a new future.[6]

With the early tillers of the soil, woman is elevated symbolically as the fecund one, the Earth Mother. Yet as a particular woman she remains the other, dominated by man. In these societies woman may be worshipped as Idol. However, she is not thereby recognized as a subject, but as Absolute other. It is *beyond* the human realm that woman's power is affirmed, not in it. Society remains male, with political power in the hands of men. Thus Beauvoir rejects the idea of an early matriarchal society. The deification of the woman by the early tillers of the soil is the result of their respect for and dependence on the fecundity of the soil, which woman through her own fecundity symbolizes. At the same time the contribution of the male to procreation is unknown. Thus the male principle is subordinated to the life principle in the symbolic representations of these people, but not so subordinated in fact.

Although she dismisses the idea of a golden age of woman as a myth, Beauvoir considers that the overthrow of the female life principle coincided with the advent of private property and the patriarchal family (recalling Engels's views on this matter), and that it brought about a much greater oppression and submergence of woman. The oppression has its roots in the will to perpetuate the family and to keep the patrimony intact. Hence woman escapes complete dependency to the degree to which she escapes the family. In a society that forbids private property and rejects the family, her position is bound to improve, although remaining subordinate.

The patriarchal family maintains its hold on women until the advent of modern industrial society, in which through labour in the factories, woman has begun to achieve her dignity as a human being. In this Beauvoir takes the side of the socialists against the individualists. She denies that abstract rights to freedom are sufficient to define the concrete situation of women. This situation is determined by women's economic role. The early individualist feminist movement lacked a concrete base for its claim to rights. It was not an autonomous movement, but partly an instrument in the hands of politicians, partly an epiphenomenon reflecting a deeper social drama. Beauvoir does not deny that equal abstract rights are necessary for women; but they must be combined with a transformed economic position. Only when economic power has fallen into the hands of the workers will working women be able to obtain the effective rights that the parasitic women of the upper and middle classes have never obtained.[7]

This hope does not alter Beauvoir's judgment that woman's liberation cannot be defined simply in terms of her becoming a liberated worker together with the abolition of the family. One of the basic problems of woman is the reconciliation of her reproductive function with her free part in productive labour. The fundamental fact which from the beginning of history doomed woman to domestic work and prevented her from participating in the formation of the human world is her enslavement to her generative function. Effective contraception, however, makes a difference. Woman can now control her pregnancies and make them a rational part of her life. She can assume her economic role, which will make her completely independent and create the possibility for the first time of full autonomy.

Beauvoir thinks that contemporary woman is still in a state of subjection. Marriage weighs much more heavily on women than on men. Women are brought up to think of their life in terms of marriage. They are less well trained and committed to a profession, do less well in it and hence value the marriage partner more. Women still ardently desire to please men. It follows that woman sees herself and makes her choices not in accordance with her true nature, but as man defines her. Yet Beauvoir feels that the game is won; that the future will bring greater and greater integration of woman into the once-masculine society. But contemporary men are deceitful in this matter. They are willing on the whole to accept woman as a fellow being and equal; but they require her at the same time to retain her femininity as the inessential other, and not to be an actor and initiator in relation to them. It must be hoped that men will accept unreservedly the situation that is coming into existence, namely women's autonomy. Only then will women be able to live without anguish.[8]

In the second part of *The Second Sex* Beauvoir explores woman's life today through a detailed analysis of her formation in modern society from her earliest years to old age. She includes analyses of basic types of women produced by this formation. These analyses have served as a model for similar exercises by subsequent feminists in understanding the character of woman as she is moulded by modern society. Rather than attempt a brief account of the various stages and elements of the analysis, I shall concentrate on particular situations of immediate relevance to the question of a changed arrangement for adult women, namely the situations of wife and mother.

According to Beauvoir the economic evolution in woman's position is turning marriage into a union freely entered into by two independent persons. But it is not yet this, and traditionally marriage has been a very different experience for man than for woman. Man is socially an independent and complete individual, first of all a producer whose existence is justified by his work. But for woman marriage is 'the only means of integration into the community. Man in marriage can harmonize transcendence and immanence, but woman in marriage has no transcendence. Contemporary marriage still reflects this duality. Yet traditional marriage is in decay. Its ideal contains a central place for the idea of home. But the home has now lost its patriarchal splendour. For the majority of men it is only a place to live in, no longer full of the memory of dead generations. The normal man regards the objects around him as instruments, while someone like the artist, who can recreate the world through his own material, is quite careless of home. Woman's work in the home remains what it has always been – cleaning, which is continuous and negative, not creative and transcendent, and cooking, which although a more positive activity does not produce durable objects.

On the whole, in Beauvoir's view, contemporary marriage is a surviving relic of dead ways of life. In it the situation of the wife is worse than before in so far as she has the same duties, but no longer the same privileges and honour. Man does not attach the same value to home. He is not contemptuous of domestic felicity, but does not treat it as an end in itself. He seeks novelty and risk, an outside life. The children do so even more, and cannot wait to escape the constraints of home.

The traditional idea of marriage is that of a community whose members have sunk their independence in the common unity. Beauvoir repudiates this ideal. The abandonment of independence means that the partners have nothing to give each other, so there results a boring and dull relation. Her ideal is for entirely self-sufficient human beings to form unions with one another only in accordance with the untrammelled dictates of their mutual love. It is for each individual alone to determine whether his will is to maintain or break the relation. Sentiment is free when it depends on no external constraints, whereas the constraints of conjugal love lead to all kinds of repressions and lies and prevent couples from knowing each other. Its daily intimacy creates neither understanding nor sympathy. But the fundamental tragedy of marriage is that it mutilates woman; it dooms her to repetition and routine. Marriage as a career for woman must be prohibited.[9]

Thus a remedy for her situation must lie in not regarding the couple as a unit. Each should be integrated as individual in society at large where he or she can flourish without aid. Then attachments would be formed between such individuals in pure generosity, founded on the acknowledgment that both are free.

In respect of her traditional function as mother, woman fulfils her physiological destiny, Beauvoir says. It is her natural calling. But human society is not wholly abandoned to nature, and the reproductive function is no longer at the mercy of biological chance. It has come under the control of human beings. Contraception together with legalized abortion would permit woman to undertake her maternity in freedom. Yet Beauvoir admits that in most cases the woman needs masculine support in accepting her responsibilities. She will gladly devote herself to her newborn child only if a man devotes himself to her. At which point Beauvoir does not tell us how the holy family is to be avoided. Maternity, however, is not a human transcendent act. The mother does not humanly create the baby, but it is made in her. As mother, woman is immanent and not free. It is then quite false to say that maternity is enough to crown a woman's life. The contemporary mother in particular is unhappy, dissatisfied and embittered. The great danger to which infants in our culture are exposed is subjection to a mother dissatisfied both sexually and socially. For maternity to be successful it must be freely assumed and sincerely wanted, and the woman must be in a position to bear the effort involved. It is desirable for the child that its mother be fulfilled in her relation to society, and it can only gain from being left less to the care of its parents and more to that of adults whose relation to it is impersonal and hence pure. In a properly organized community, then, children would be taken in charge for the most part by the community, the mother would be cared for and helped, and maternity would cease to be incompatible with careers for women.

Beauvoir ends her work with an account of her idea of the independent and autonomous woman. In the first place she reiterates the criticism of civil liberties as insufficient without economic freedom. Nothing less than gainful employment can guarantee her liberty. But in the second place the mere combination of a vote and a job is not sufficient for woman's emancipation, since on account of the socio-economic structure work today is not liberty. Even socialized labour is not sufficient. For the successful professional woman still has problems arising from the duality of her destiny as woman and as human being. As woman she is required to realize the ideal of femininity, and be passive object to man as active subject. She cannot renounce her sexual nature without mutilation and cannot fulfil it without conforming to the sexual values of man. Hence a further condition of woman's liberation is the transformation of these values. The act of love itself must become a free exchange in which ideas of victory and defeat are abandoned.

Men and women today, Beauvoir thinks, are dissatisfied with each other. But this is not necessary. There is no eternal hostility between male and female. The hostility arises from woman's envy of and desire for the transcendence which man enjoys. She seeks to escape from her prison and man lets her go with bad grace. She replies with an aggressive attitude, and instead of mutual recognition as free beings each wishes to dominate the other.

A world in which men and women would be equal is easy to envisage, according to Beauvoir. It is precisely what the Soviet Revolution promised. Women reared and trained exactly like men to work under the same conditions and for the same rewards; marriage based on free agreement; maternity made voluntary through free contraception and abortion; state care of children, not in the sense of removing them from, but of not abandoning them to, their parents. Such a world, Beauvoir concludes, would not be an androgynous one. There would always remain certain differences between men and women. In particular woman's eroticism and her sexual world have a special form of their own.[10]

The Proto-Radical Feminists

Beauvoir's work is an analysis of all the difficulties that prevent woman from achieving her nature as a fully free and creative being. A major element in her analysis is the idea that woman's feminine nature as passive object is the creation of man in his project to realize his freedom. But at the same time we find in Beauvoir's work evidence against such a view. Beauvoir constantly emphasizes that it is woman's biological function as mother and consequent role as child-rearer and home-minder which imposes a passivity on her, because it is an existence concerned with the continuity and renewal of life, and not with active freedom. In these respects it is not man's project that defines woman's passivity; at most one could say that man builds up the passive elements in woman's existence into a fixed conception of her nature and that it is this image that is imposed on her. Indeed Beauvoir acknowledges in the end that there is an opposition in woman between her sexual nature and her human nature, an opposition that is not present in man. But her paradoxical conclusion is that woman's sexual nature can be changed. Woman can be liberated from the prison of traditional marriage and the family home, and by becoming, like man, active in her sexual nature can fulfil herself as human and sexual being.

In the great outburst of feminist thought and activity of the late 1960s, it was not, however, Beauvoir's work which had the immediate impact so much as the less radical and penetrating thought of Friedan. I have already discussed Friedan's *The Feminine Mystique* as a later example of individualist feminism. Here it may be mentioned again in connection with the developing inquiry into the man-made nature of the feminine character. Her work is an explanation and criticism of the image of woman's nature as feminine and thus one which is not autonomous and creative but passive and appropriately fulfilled in the roles of wife and mother. Friedan shows how the worlds of education, psychoanalysis, sociology and advertising have combined to re-implant this idea in the new generation of women, with the consequence that they cannot enjoy an active life outside the home without feeling guilt at the neglect of their true function and at the loss of their femininity. However, Friedan's powerful appeal to women to liberate themselves from this image and to seek an active life, does not involve, as was noted in the first chapter, a repudiation of women's responsibility for child and home, but calls for a reconciliation of their sexual and human nature within the nuclear family and individualist society. Thus she implicitly accepts a differentiated sexual nature for men and women besides their common human nature.

It is in the writers of the 1970s that we find the extreme version of the idea that femininity is man's creation of woman in his own interests. An early example of this idea, which does not, however, draw the social and political conclusions that form a usual part of the full radical feminist position, is Eva Figes's book *Patriarchal Attitudes*. She begins by saying that her researches have not yielded a conclusive answer on the fundamental question of secondary sexual differences, by which she means the sexual differentiation of human behaviour and ability. She first admits that scientific research on the issue has been inconclusive or has tended to support the view that secondary sexual differences are the product of nurture rather than nature. But she immediately interprets this to mean that there is almost no evidence in favour of the nature hypothesis and overwhelming evidence in favour of nurture. This allows her to proceed on the assumption that women have been largely man-made, and to investigate the attitudes of men to women through which this making has been carried on. But I think Figes would hardly claim that her few comments on the scientific evidence were a serious consideration of the issues. She refers to the view that a difference in hormone level between adult men and women partly explains the sexual differentiation of behaviour, but rejects it on the grounds that there is no difference of hormone level in boys and girls aged four to five years who already show marked behaviour differences. Besides this reference she appeals to the work of anthropologists which emphasizes the importance of sexual role-playing in the differentiation of the sexes.[11] It must be said that this question deserves more extended treatment, and if the results are inconclusive, it cannot be reasonable to treat them as conclusive.

In the body of her work Figes is largely concerned with the intellectual world, the worlds of morality, philosophy, psychoanalysis and religion. She explores these areas for the way in which the images of women contained in them express the view of woman as different and inferior in nature. We may note Figes's conclusion that woman must above all be liberated from marriage, which makes her an appendage to man, with the corollary that children are to become the primary responsibility of the state.

An important element in the formation of radical feminist thought was the New Left movement. Many radical feminists acknowledge this influence and were in fact New Left radicals before they became radical feminists. The New Left was a collection of black and student protest movements, originating in America but influential throughout Europe, which sprang from the vague anarchist interpretation of Marx's notion of alienation.[12] The basic situation faced by the thinkers who influenced the movement was the failure of the working class in advanced capitalist countries to become revolutionary. Instead, the workers had improved their position and been integrated politically, socially and economically in capitalist society. To preserve in these conditions something of the Marxist faith required an abandonment of those parts of the theory which emphasize the materialist and objective factors making for revolution, and an invention of others which would explain the failure of the working class to become revolutionary. A major figure in this reconstruction was Herbert Marcuse. The particular significance of

Marcuse for the development of radical feminism consists in the fact that his explanation of the persistence of capitalism involves a radical modification of Freudian psychology, in which capitalist repression is linked with sexual repression in the family. The overcoming of capitalist repression calls for a general sexual liberation which would reject the traditional sexual structure of male and female roles in all its forms.

But before considering Marcuse, we should refer briefly to a much earlier thinker who developed similar ideas and who continues to be read in the contemporary period by feminists. This is Wilhelm Reich. Reich was an Austrian who was both a psychoanalyst and member of the Austrian Communist party in 1920. It was Reich who invented the term 'sexual politics', which was later taken over by the radical feminists. In his book *The Sexual Revolution* he is concerned with the struggle between freedom and authority, and writes from the point of view of an advocate of man's complete liberation from all structures of authority. While he espouses a communist position and sees the abolition of capitalism as a necessary condition of human liberation, he does not accept the basic Marxist position that the root of authoritarian structures lies in the relation of men to the means of production. His view is that their root lies in psychic structures formed in the individual in the process of his sexual development in the family. The cause of abnormal psychic reactions which produce authoritarian psychic and social structures is misdirected and unsatisfied sexual energy. Sexual energy governs the structure of human feeling and thinking. It is the life energy itself.[13]

In his explanation of the undesirable repressions of sexual energy in the family, Reich draws on Freud's theory. In particular he identifies the crucial period at which repressive psychic structures begin to be formed in the individual as the time when the child, aged four to five years, first experiences a conflict between instinctual life energy and the demands of morality as expressed by the father and incorporated into the child in the form of the superego. The further development of the moral demands that the individual makes on himself increases the damming up of his sexual energy. In this conflict between the individual's life energy and moral authority, which Reich represents also as one between the ego and the outer world, the organism is forced to protect

111

itself both against its own life force and against the outer world.

The trouble with Freud, in Reich's view, is his claim that civilization depends on instinctual repression. For Reich the truth is that repression is the basis only of a patriarchal authoritarian civilization. Freud sees that instinctual renunciation by the child produces a neurosis which renders the individual anti-social and incapable of cultural development. But Freud proposes to cure the neurosis by bringing it to consciousness and sublimating the repressed energy in some form of civilized activity. For Reich however this process of liberating oneself from the incest wish by sublimating and controlling it does not liberate one from sexuality and its needs. These remain unsatisfied.

On Reich's view morality is the cause of the anti-social impulses of the unconscious. The unconscious itself is socially determined. Morality arose when an upper class arose and acquired an economic interest in suppressing natural needs. Once moral repression had created the anti-social impulses, it produced its own justification. But it continues to be needed only so long as a natural regulation of life energies has not yet succeeded. Such a natural regulation would constitute a new sexuo-economic morality.

The traditional family is the basis of the authoritarian morality and the means of its transmission to successive generations. The family is itself the result of specific economic constellations, in particular of class society founded on private property. The family serves as a factory for producing authoritarian ideologies and structures. The triangular structure of the family determines this effect. In the Oedipus or Electra complex the child directs its first genital love to the parent of the opposite sex and feels hatred and jealousy for the other and this engenders guilt feelings in it. This repression can be avoided only if the child is brought up from its third year together with other children and without the influence of parent fixation. It would then develop an entirely different sexuality. The elimination of the parent fixation is the central requirement. Its continued presence can ruin an otherwise collective education, as when the young child spends several hours a day in nursery or kindergarten. The child is oppressed by parental authority on the basis of its physical smallness alone, quite apart from the parents' moral oppression of the child. Hence the abolition of the family and the disappearance of this oppression is

112

the pre-requisite of a healthy sexual life. The family has served only to reproduce itself by crippling people sexually, and has the political function of creating individuals who are afraid of life and of authority, and who can thus be governed by a handful of powerful men.[14]

Traditional marriage, then, which Reich calls compulsive or formal marriage, must be abolished, and natural marriage, by which Reich means a sexual union maintained solely at the partners' will, must replace it. The social prerequisite of natural marriage is the economic independence of the woman, the social care and education of children, and the total absence of interference in the union of considerations of economic interest. Reich says that lasting sexual unions are to be preferred to temporary ones on the grounds that they are necessary to produce complete sensual adaptation between partners. However, by a lasting union he does not mean a lifelong attachment to one person, which he considers to be sexuo-economically impossible, but a relation that may last as little as a few weeks. There is to be in any case complete freedom to enjoy other partners in such natural marriages.

Reich's explanation of the failure of the socialist revolution to achieve a complete human liberation is of relevance to feminism, because the explanation is centred on the role of the patriarchal, male-dominated family. This opens up the possibility of explaining the subordination of woman from a point of view which is not hostile to socialism and its ideals, and which emphasizes not the class war between men, but the sexual relation within the family. It makes the absence of a free sexual relation between men and women the basis of all authoritarian structures, including those within socialist society.

Herbert Marcuse was also of central European origin, and migrated to America in the 1930s. In his work Freudian theory was used to supplement a socialist notion of human liberation of more immediate influence on contemporary feminism. In *Eros and Civilization* Marcuse follows Reich's criticism of Freud's view that human instincts must be sacrificed for the sake of civilization. He admits that this sacrifice has paid off well in terms of material progress, but not in terms of human freedom. On the contrary the domination of man by man has been constantly increasing. And, like Reich, he finds within Freud's theory reasons for rejecting the belief in the necessity of instinctual repression. The repressive civilization has itself created the preconditions for the gradual abolition of repression.[15]

On Freud's theory, according to Marcuse, the unconscious, ruled by the pleasure principle, strives for nothing but pleasure, but man has to learn to renounce immediate pleasure, and adopt the reality principle. In this way the individual becomes an organized rational ego. The replacement of the pleasure principle by the reality principle is the great traumatic event in the history of the race and of the individual. Yet the unconscious retains the objectives of the defeated pleasure principle. It retains the immediate identification of freedom and happiness. Thus the possibility remains, in Marcuse's view, for a re-cognition of this hidden past which will explode the rationality of the repressed individual and become the vehicle for future liberation.

The repressive modification of instincts is enforced and sustained by the primordial struggle for existence as a result of scarcity. But it is not so much in the restraints of the ego that Marcuse in the end identifies the origins of the repressed individual, as in the development of the superego. The superego originates from dependency on the parents, whose external restrictions on the child are absorbed into the ego and become its conscience. It enforces the demands of reality on the individual, but also the demands of a past reality, the external restrictions of childhood. It is in the bitter adjustment to these demands, Marcuse holds, that unfreedom is accepted.

In rejecting Freud's claim that civilization necessarily involves repression Marcuse distinguishes between a basic repression necessary for any civilization and a surplus repression which consists in additional restraints necessitated by the social domination of some by others. Basic repression, which is the power to restrain and guide instinctual drives and make biological necessities into individual needs and desires, increases rather than reduces gratification. Surplus repression involves additional restraints on instinctual drives necessary only for the social control of resources in the interests of a particular group. Its primary mechanism is that of the monogamic patriarchal family. This involves the repressive organization of sexuality so that from an autonomous principle governing the entire organism it is turned into the specialized temporary function of procreation.[16] Freud believed, according to Marcuse, that unless this channelling of sexuality into monogamic institutions was carried through, all civilized non-sexual relations would be made impossible. Yet Freud admits, Marcuse says, that eros itself seeks to create larger unities.

Social domination, Marcuse believes, has been so successful in expanding man's control over nature, that scarcity is no longer a convincing justification of repression. The poverty in the world is not due to scarcity but to the manner in which resources are used and distributed. However, the closer technology brings the possibility of liberation from the constraints required by scarcity, the more the established order feels the need to maintain these constraints. Thus totalitarian control develops for the sake of keeping people mobilized and distracted from the real situation. At the same time, because collective social control has become much more effective, the role of the family and of sexual repression ceases to be so important. The individual no longer needs a superego developed in the family as he has become a technical tool of society.[17]

Marcuse then turns to the idea of a non-repressive civilization. Through the rational organization of fully developed industrial society, scarcity will have been conquered and all individual needs can be fulfilled. Basic human needs would be satisfied without toil or alienated labour because of the automization of labour. The quantum of instinctual energy directed to necessary labour would be so small that large areas of repressive constraints would collapse, and the antagonistic relation between the pleasure principle and the reality principle would be altered in favour of the former. Eros could be released to an unprecedented degree.[18]

Instinctual liberation would, however, still be compatible with socially useful work and civilization. Work would be enjoyed, but it would be outside the sphere of work in artistic creation that the new freedom would be realized. The aesthetic function operating through the play impulse would abolish compulsion and place man morally and physically in a state of freedom.

The liberated sex instincts would develop a libidinal rationality which would promote progress to a higher rationality. It would involve the re-sexualization of the whole body and eroticization of the whole personality. The patriarchal family would simply disintegrate and disappear. The released libido would nevertheless sublimate itself in lasting and expanding relations between individuals who would cultivate their environment together for their developing needs and faculties. This self-sublimation would serve to intensify and enlarge instinctual gratification. It would be a sensuous rationality which contained its own moral laws, on the content of which Marcuse fails to enlighten us.[19]

In a later work, *One Dimensional Man*, Marcuse criticizes Western civilization in terms of a notion of transcendent reason which gives us knowledge of the true nature of freedom, beauty, joy of living and so on.[20] He still appeals, however, to a future that will create a universal eros and a libidinous civilization. The revolution, which will bring this about, will be made by a substratum of outcasts and outsiders, the exploited and persecuted of other races, the unemployed, the radical students. Marcuse's vision held out the promise of a world of unrestrained energy, liberated from all repressive discipline, and unlimited by the need for productive labour. Of particular relevance for the feminist is the connection in Marcuse's thought, as in Reich's, between the repressive structures of existing civilization and the sexual repression of the patriarchal family.

Germaine Greer (b. 1939)

Greer's book *The Female Eunuch* was one of those feminist works published in 1970 which caught the general attention and made a considerable if temporary impact. Her basic idea is that conveyed in the title. Woman as traditionally conceived is a passive sexual being. The truth in this is that she has been castrated by man. Her real sexual nature and whole personality is to be as active and adventurous as any man.

Greer acknowledges the influence of the New Left as the forcing house of the contemporary feminist movement,[21] though she admits that the aims of the latter movement are unclear and unspecific. It stands for liberation through revolution, but what that revolution involves is vague. It does mean, however, that women should not enter into marriage: they should be promiscuous and self-sufficient. She admits the irresponsibility of these ideas, but justifies it on the grounds that it is the very will to live, and above all to live sexually, that women must recover. The new way of life must be joyous and full of energy. We cannot now see what is ultimately desirable for women, and so no ultimate strategy can be designed, but women's first task is to devise their own mode of revolt. To do this they must reassess themselves and discover how they have been falsely made, and hence what their true nature is.[22]

The primary question for Greer, as for Figes, is then that of the natural inferiority or dependence of women. Unless we know that women are no different from men we cannot make out a case for female liberation, she thinks. Hence we must begin by questioning the most basic assumptions about feminine normality in order to reopen possibilities of development at present blocked off by social and ideological conditioning.[23] The assumption behind the discussion, Greer says, is that everything we may observe about female behaviour could be otherwise.

Following many other feminists Greer attacks the idea of the Eternal Feminine, the stereotype of woman – the dominant image of femininity which, she thinks, rules our culture and to which all women aspire. The particular twist that Greer gives to her attack is the idea of the sexlessness of the image. The value of woman lies solely in the demand she excites in others. She has simply to be lovely and passive, a doll, an idol whose essential quality is castratedness. She must be young, her body hairless, her flesh buoyant, and without a sexual organ.[24] The basic evil of this image consists in the repression of sexual energy which it involves. This repression affects the rest of woman's life and activity outside the home, where she has always to take the second place. She is less original, curious, and energetic than man. Thus the castration is not a narrowly sexual one, since sexual energy is conceived in Freudian fashion as the life energy itself.

To understand the creation of this castrated feminine woman we must begin with the pressures which form her from the cradle onwards. The baby has an enormous natural curiosity, but Greer believes, with Reich and Marcuse, that our family arrangements involve a massive psychic repression. The family environment of the baby consists overwhelmingly in the figure of the mother, in whom the baby becomes absorbed. It acquires a sense of its ego in the difference between its own and its mother's desires, and this ego-consciousness becomes the basis for an egoistic morality in which restraints are first of all imposed on the ego by external authority, and then integrated into the personality to form the self-repressing superego.

The repression of psychic energy in the traditional family occurs both in boys and girls, but the more particular repression of female energy begins through the discrimination of the girl by type of dress and colour, and by the restriction of her behaviour to less adventurous and more home-bound activities, and by her introduction to menial roles and household skills. At primary school, it is true, the girl is given the same education as the boy apart from some female frills such as cooking. But it is at puberty that the girl learns to become a eunuch by giving up her autonomy, seeking guidance from others and in general adopting a passive attitude.

The modern nuclear family must, therefore, be abolished. It is too small, self-contained and self-centred. Greer combines, following Reich and Marcuse, the Freudian with the Marxist critique of the patriarchal family as rooted in the male interest in the inheritance of private property by his legitimate offspring. But this does not stop her from praising an older form of the patriarchal family: the so-called stem family in which different generations as well as siblings inhabit and work the same property. In such a family the mother is not isolated, and the mother-child relation does not become an anti-social one. Greer wishes to capture something of the spirit of such a communal life in her idea for the replacement of the nuclear family by what she calls organic families, in which the children would not all come from the same parents, nor would all parents or mothers live permanently in the family home. Women would contribute children and visit from time to time. Children, Greer thinks, are more disturbed by changes of place than by changes in those caring for them. The point of such a system of multiple care would be to release the children from the burden of being the extension of their parents, so that they can belong primarily to themselves. At the same time she thinks that they will become better members of a community because they will have developed a sense of their continuity with others.[25] The uncertainty in these ideas – whether the child should belong primarily to itself or to others – is as evident in Greer as it was in Gilman.

With the abolition of the nuclear family would go also the life-long monogamous marriage. Greer thinks, like Reich, that it is absurd to pledge oneself for life. But this does not involve a rejection of the ideal of love. Love is a relation between equals, in which each sees in the other the image of oneself and loves it as oneself. This love is the basis of community of all kinds from the smallest to the largest. The state, however, is not such a community. It has no common good, and is held together only by an external and repressive discipline.[26] As against this ideal love Greer draws an unpleasing picture of the middle-class myth of romantic love as the basis of marriage. Romantic love is an egoism à deux in which the loving couple conceive their unity as something which must be protected and enforced against others. It is also represented as a mutual dependence of the partners, when the ideal of love must aim at the independence of each.[27] Once again Greer betrays an uncertainty as to the relation of self to others, in this case a confusion as to whether a truly loving couple constitute a genuine unity in themselves, which must necessarily involve both the exclusion of others and mutual dependence, or whether the couple remain independent and uncommitted individuals.

Greer, like Friedan, speaks about and to the frustrations of the educated middle-class woman, who is expected to fulfil the traditional woman's role and ideal of femininity, whatever else she may do outside the home. But, unlike Friedan, her emphasis is on liberating the sexuality of woman. Friedan, she argues, in wishing to reduce the importance of the traditional sex-role of woman as mother is forced to stress the non-sexual elements of woman's being at the expense of her libido. Women should not become simply additional men, dominated by the authority of reason. They must develop their sexuality and express it in their whole personalities.

The chief means of liberating women is to replace compulsive and compelled behaviour by the pleasure principle. In marriage and the family the activities of cooking, housekeeping and attention to personal appearance, are all compulsive activities. But it is possible to engage in these activities for pleasure. The essence of pleasure is spontaneity. Spontaneity means the rejection of norms, and the following of self-regulating principles. We are afraid that such liberty will bring chaos but we must face the insecurity. We do not know what a new and free sexual regime will be like, but we must be willing to experiment. Women cannot wait for the socialist revolution, they must revolt now, for they are the most oppressed class. But women's liberation, by destroying the patriarchal family, will destroy the necessary substructure of the authoritarian state, and once that withers away we will have socialism.[28]

Radical Feminism

In Greer's book there is a section entitled 'Hate', which begins with the assertion that women have very little idea of how much men hate them and proceeds to a catalogue of such hate as it is expressed in male attitudes to the sexual act itself, in rape, verbal abuse and post-coital disgust. Yet for Greer man as such is not the enemy who has castrated women. In so far as Greer has a general explanation of woman's oppression, it is that the nuclear family rooted in private property does the castrating. At the same time Greer is not calling for women's participation in a socialist revolution which will liberate the workers and themselves together. Her call is for women as a class to revolt. This idea of women as a class, indeed as the most oppressed class, is an essential element in the fully-fledged position of radical feminism. However, it has to be completed by an account of men as the ruling class and of a political order through which men's rule over women is constituted. We do not find such an account in Greer's book, but with Kate Millett's work *Sexual Politics*[29] these ideas are given expression.

Millett says that she is concerned with the theory of sexual politics. By politics she means a power-relationship in which one group of persons is controlled by another. The relation between the sexes now and throughout history is an instance of such dominance. Males rule females by right of birth, and their rule has been so effective and durable and its nature largely unexamined, because it has involved an interior colonization of the subject people. The sexual dominion of males over females, Millett claims, is the most pervasive ideology of our culture and constitutes the most fundamental structure of power in our society. This society she calls a patriarchy. All historical societies, indeed, have been patriarchies. A patriarchy is a society in which the half of the populace that is female is controlled by the half that is male. The principles of patriarchy are twofold: (1) male shall dominate female, (2) older male shall dominate younger. Millett admits that patriarchy exhibits a great variety of forms. But in all such forms avenues of power are in male hands. Sexual politics, then, is the politics of patriarchy. It obtains consent through the socialization of both sexes in accordance with the required temperament, role and status. Temperament is determined by the formation of the human personality according to sexual stereotypes, which are based on the needs and values of the dominant group. It is complemented by the notion of a sex-role involving codes of conduct appropriate to each sex. In this social differentiation of identity the more limited role given to females arrests them at the level of biological experience of sex and maternity while distinctively human experience is reserved for the male. The distinction of status between male and female follows from such an assignment of roles.[30]

Patriarchal religion, popular attitudes and, to some degree, science assumes that these psychosocial distinctions rest on biological differences. Hence the claim always made that culture cooperates with nature to produce the sexual differentiation of human beings. But Millett argues that the scientific evidence does not support this claim. Attempts to prove that temperamental dominance is inherent in the male have been notably unsuccessful, she thinks. The evidence on the whole supports the view that gender or sexual-personality structure is overwhelmingly cultural in character. At birth there is a common psycho-sexual nature, while the basic elements of gender identity are established by the age of eighteen months. We will, in any case, hardly be in a position to find out what real differences in the sexes exist until we reduce the cultural differences between them. But this apparent agnosticism does not represent her position, since she is evidently committed to the rejection of the claim that there is a sexually differentiated human nature.[31]

Since patriarchy's biological foundations appear so very insecure, she admits that one has cause to admire the strength of a socialization which can maintain a universal condition on faith alone. It is the conditioning of early childhood, which develops aggression in the male and thwarts it in the female, that is decisive. Under the aegis of such artificially engendered masculine and feminine personalities each person realizes little more than half his potential. But of more political significance is that this leads to a power or status division.

Patriarchy's chief institution is the family. The family is a mirror of the larger society and connects the individual with it. As the fundamental instrument and foundation unit of patriarchal society, the family, with its sexually differentiated roles, is prototypical. The main contribution of the family to the support of patriarchy consists in the socialization of the young as described above. The family is maintained, Millett holds, by the principle of legitimacy, which is the requirement that no child shall be brought into the world without one man having the role of father. Although there is no biological reason why reproduction and socialization should occur in the family, the retention of these functions in the family, she says, has been the basic pattern of all historical societies, and hence testifies to the success of the principle of legitimacy. Revolutionary or utopian efforts to remove the functions from the family have been frustrated, and most experiments have involved a gradual return to the tradition. This is strong evidence, Millett says, of how basic a form in all societies patriarchy is, and how influential on the family members. She concludes that attempts to alter this pattern in a radical way without a thorough understanding of the family as a socio-political institution will not be productive.[32]

A basic claim of radical feminists is that women constitute an oppressed class. Consequently they have to deny that women merely take on the class status of their husbands and fathers. Superficially they do assume this status, Millett says, but in the final analysis women tend to transcend the usual class stratifications in patriarchy because the female has fewer class associations than the male. Economic dependence on husband or father make her affiliations with any class a tangential, vicarious and temporary matter. Not only do women constitute an oppressed class, but this sexual class division of society is more important in determining the general character of society than class divisions based on property ownership and control. This does not mean that revolutionary socialism is repudiated, but only that priority morally, socially and politically is given to the oppression of females by males over the oppression of some males by others.[33]

One of the most efficient branches of patriarchal government, Millett claims, is that through which an economic hold is obtained over its female subjects. In traditional patriarchies women are non-persons without legal standing and can neither own property nor earn a living. In contemporary patriarchy women have rights, but they are still economically subordinate, firstly because they are not paid for the work they do in the home, and secondly because they are restricted to inferior employment opportunities and rewards.

Like Greer, Millett notes a widespread masculine hostility to females which is expressed in pornographic literature and satire. She argues that such hostility is functional within patriarchy. The male's sexual antipathy provides a means of control over a subordinate group, and a rationale for that group's inferior status. Millett notes in particular the importance in this hostility of what she calls men's house culture, pure male activities such as hunting, war or sport. The tone and ethos of this culture, she claims, is sadistic, power-oriented, latently homosexual and misogynist.

Patriarchy's greatest psychological weapon, according to Millett, is its universality and longevity. A referent for the feminist revolution scarcely exists. Yet she believes that when the workings of a system of power are exposed and questioned, the system becomes not only subject to discussion, but to change also. She believes that we are in such a period.

The overthrow of patriarchy requires a complete sexual revolution which would destroy the traditional taboos on homosexuality, bastardy, adolescent and pre- and extra-marital sex – in other words there should be unrestricted sexual activity of all kinds. Monogamous marriage would not survive such freedom, and with it would go the patriarchal family authority, which is the basis of the patriarchal state. To replace the family, professional collective care of the young would have to be developed, but Millett believes, like all other feminists opposed to the family, that this would involve an improvement in child care. That the care and education of children become a public matter, Millett claims, is an absolutely basic condition of female liberation. So long as every female is obliged by anatomy to be the primary caretaker of childhood, she is prevented from becoming a human being.[34]

Instead of the family, collective care; instead of monogamous marriage, conceived by Millett in Reichian terms as compulsive, the voluntary sexual association. How is this revolution to come about? Primarily in human consciousness through the destruction of the ideology of male supremacy and its traditional forms of socialization. The changes in women's position that have taken place in the twentieth century in both liberal and socialist societies, Millett says, have altered institutions, but not habits of mind. Although women have acquired equal rights, it was not realized how deep the patriarchal ideology went, and how little such formal changes would alter women's real position. This shows, Millett thinks, that the primary social and political distinctions are not those based on wealth or rank, but those based on sex.

Engels in his work on the origins of the family, Millett claims, recognizes that the possession of women by men was the first class-oppression, which brings with it all the others. Millett characterizes it as the keystone to the total structure of human injustice. This is not actually Engels's position, since for him the oppression of women is the consequence of private property and the male interest in legitimate heirs, but it is precisely the radical feminist position.

In Shulamith Firestone's book *The Dialectic of Sex* we find another attempt to theorize the idea that the basic class division and oppression in society is the sexual one.[35] The weakness of Millett's position consists in the absence in it of any account of how patriarchy arises, and in the simple appeal to human consciousness to end it. Firestone grasps this difficulty without hesitation. She sees that if radical feminism is to constitute an alternative class analysis to the Marxist one, it must provide an historical explanation of women's oppression and of its successive transformations and final supersession in a liberated future, which can compete with Marxist theory. Firestone is nothing if not ambitious. She intends to include the Marxist theory of the oppression of workers within the more comprehensive theory of sex oppression, and she wants to use the Marxist conception of dialectic and materialism to do this. By dialectic she means a view of the world as a process in which a natural flux of action and reaction understood as irreconcilable opposites occurs. Her theory is materialist, she thinks, because it traces the constitution of economic classes and political society to organic causes. Firestone contrasts the utopianism of other feminists with her own dialectical materialist theory of sex. In this she imitates Marx and Engels, who criticized earlier socialist thinkers for their utopian positing of an ideal world of equality to be produced by thought without being able to show how such a world was being produced in reality.

Her first premise is that there is a level of reality which is not directly economic, and which she calls psycho-sexual reality. Firestone develops this premise in criticism of Beauvoir, whose work she nevertheless treats as hitherto the most profound analysis of woman's position. Fundamental to Beauvoir is the category of otherness. The subjection of women springs from the necessity of consciousness to posit and subject the other. Yet if this is fundamental, Firestone asks, why does Beauvoir feel the need to go on to show the biological and historical circumstances which have pushed women into such a category? The much more likely possibility is that the fundamental male/female dualism springs from sex itself. Biology, or procreation, is at the bottom of this dualism. The immediate assumption of the layman that the unequal division of the sexes is grounded in nature may be well founded. Having raised this possibility, Firestone goes on to assert without qualification that men and women were created differently, and that the reproductive functions of these differences created a class system. The biological family involves an inherently unequal distribution of power. It is the psycho-sexual formation of each individual in accordance with this imbalance which leads to the development of classes.[36]

The biological family has the following characteristics: (1) prior to the development of methods of birth-control women are at the continual mercy of biology, which makes them dependent on males for physical survival; (2) infants are dependent on adults for survival; (3) the basic interdependence of mother and child shapes the psychology of every mature female and infant; (4) natural reproductive differences lead directly to the first division of labour based on sex which was the origin of all further

125

division into economic classes.

The biological family has existed everywhere. Yet to admit that the sexual imbalance of power is biologically based is not to abandon the case for women's liberation. Human beings are not animals. We can get rid of the family. The underclass must revolt and seize control of the means of reproduction, by which she means the new technology for artificial reproduction in test-tubes, as well as the social institutions of child-rearing. The goal of the revolt is the elimination of the sex distinction itself, by which she means, not the elimination of men, but the disappearance of the attribution of any significance to genital differences. There would be pan-sexuality and androgynous people, no men and women. Reproduction would be through artificial means, child-care in group forms – which would apparently end the subordination of children to adults – and finally, for good measure, labour would be abolished through the cybernation of work. With the abolition of the family would go the psychology of power in which economic classes are grounded.[37]

It is evident, then, that Firestone does not really believe that men and women have sexually differentiated natures. Her position is that biology produces the family and the family produces masculine and feminine. Since through technology we can eliminate the biological basis of the family, we can thereby eliminate masculine and feminine and produce androgynous people. She thus shares the view of Millett that it is the family that is at the centre of the formation of the sexually differentiated personalities in which power, class and domination are grounded, and also that it is through the abolition of the family that these injustices are to be removed. The distinguishing feature of her position is that she provides an explanation for the existence of the family and an explanation of how the material conditions for its supersession are being produced.

Historical materialism à la Firestone, then, is the view that the course of history is determined by the division of society into distinct biological classes for procreative reproduction, and by the struggles of these classes with one another; by the changes in the modes of marriage, reproduction and child-care created by these struggles, and by the first division of labour based on sex which developed into the economic class system.[38]

126

Firestone also needs an account of how the biological family creates in men the desire for power. She has suggested simply that it produces an imbalance in power by making women dependent on men. But in order to build the whole oppressive class system on such a conception she needs to show that men are not satisfied with a limited power, but become power-hungry. For this purpose she adopts a version of the radical Freudianism of Reich and Marcuse. Firestone believes that Freud observed correctly the psychological structures of men and women, and understood also that they were the consequences of the incest taboo, which was itself necessary for the preservation of the family. The consequent early sexual repression of the child is the basic mechanism whereby the character structures of individuals which support political, ideological and economic serfdom are produced. By getting rid of the incest taboo and the family at the same time it will be possible for a pan-sexuality, which corresponds to the initial diffuseness of the sex drive at birth, to eroticize the whole culture[39]

Firestone thinks that children share in women's oppression. Like their mothers, they are dependent for their survival on patronage, and this is in itself an oppressive state to be in. But in modern society the position of children is peculiarly oppressive. Following the work of the social historian P. Ariès she thinks of the social distinction of childhood as an invention of modern times.[40] In the Middle Ages children had no cultural identity as such. They were tiny adults with responsibilities as servants or apprentices, and thus were not so heavily dependent on their parents. The consequence of the invention of childhood has been the separation of children from adult life, their segregation in special institutions, the cultivation of special value for them, all of which, she argues, serves to retard their development and continue their dependence on adults. In a society free of exploitation, in which the problem of work would have been conquered by cybernetics, children would become self-regulating and hence free. Thus in the free society of the future the problem of childcare would have been greatly reduced. In so far as it remains, Firestone holds, the care of children is no more the responsibility of the mother than that of anyone else – an assumption, she says, that is basic to the revolutionary demands of radical feminism.[41]

Like Greer, Firestone attempts to distinguish between true

love which involves an equality between the lovers and is thus impossible between men and women in contemporary society because of the inequality in power between them, and romantic love, which is love perverted by the context of power. Romantic love is a cultural tool of male supremacy for keeping women, who are potentially free, from knowing their true condition.

The most apocalyptic element in Firestone's work is her vision of the world transformed by the new techniques of production. Following Marcuse she predicts the disappearance of male-dominated scientific and technological culture through its fusion with the aesthetic mode of experience. There will be a total understanding of the laws of nature and a complete mastery of nature so that culture as traditionally conceived will no longer be necessary. There will be the full realization of the conceivable in the actual, and hence the control and delay of the satisfaction of libidinal impulses by the ego will be unnecessary. Revolutionary ecology will be developed in which an artificial man-made balance replaces the natural one. Machines will take over the work of society, and human activity will become play. To bring about these fantasies a feminist revolution is necessary.[42]

The feminist revolution will be the ultimate one. It involves: (1) the liberation of women from the tyranny of reproductive biology, and the diffusion of the child-bearing and child-rearing role to society as a whole; (2) the full self-determination of women and children. This requires their economic independence. A feminist socialism, according to Firestone, will involve an equal distribution of wealth to children; (3) the total integration of women and children into all aspects of the larger society; (4) the freedom of women and children to do whatever they wish sexually.

In the new society ownership would be in the hands of society, and wealth would be distributed on the basis of needs. Living arrangements would consist of flexible group households with adults and children having rights of transfer to other households. The activity of men and women would then consist solely in the pursuit of specialized interests for their own sake.[43]

Radical feminism is self-evidently the most extreme form of feminism. It alone attaches no value whatsoever to the differentia-

tion of the sexes, which, apart from its physical form in the sexual
organs and other possible physical characteristics, it sees as something not determined biologically, but by and in the interests of
men. Furthermore, it alone sees *all* traditional social order as
founded on the domination of women by men. Given these
beliefs, it seemed for many radical feminists that they must have
as little as possible to do with men, and that in the sphere of
sexual relations only relations with other women were compatible
with their fundamental position. Hence for such feminists lesbianism came to be a touchstone of the true faith: 'feminism is the
theory: lesbianism is the practice', as the slogan attributed to Ti
Grace Atkinson put it.[44]

Since the basic idea of radical feminism is that there should be
no sexual role differentiation between men and women in any
sphere whatever, then it indeed follows that there cannot be such
a differentiation in the sphere of sexual intercourse itself, and
hence the heterosexual relation cannot be the appropriate norm.
But neither, as A. de Koedt argues, can lesbianism be the norm
for women. From the point of view of radical feminism any
sexual relation must be as good as any other, for the difference
between men and women in sex, as in everything else, must cease
to be significant. One should be concerned not with sex between
men and women, or sex between women only, but with sex
among persons, for whom the mere fact of a male or female body
is an irrelevant accident. Those women who wish to make lesbianism a condition of authentic feminism, Koedt says, mis-
takenly identify man as such as the enemy, whereas it is only man
in so far as he adopts the male supremacist role who is the enemy.
As a person identical in nature to women as persons, a man as
sexual partner or as anything else is as such neither better nor
worse than a woman. Women are not to be identified by their
relation to other women, which would give them a sexual
identity, but by their nature as autonomous beings, who are
defined by their own particular achievements and characteristics.

The total abolition of sexual roles in society would involve the
coming into existence of what the radical feminists call an androgynous world. By this they mean that the differentiation of men
and women into masculine and feminine characters and sensibilities, being a product of patriarchal society and not something

biologically based, will disappear with the abolition of the different sexual roles of that society. Sexual anatomy will be irrelevant to who one is, what one does, and with whom one makes love.[45]

Radical Feminism and Socialist Feminism

Radical feminism appears to be a complete social and political theory in itself, since it purports to explain the social and political order in terms of the power relations between men and women. But its inadequacy in this respect is immediately obvious. It contains no conception particular to itself of the nature of the individual and of his relations to others in a community. In fact what radical feminism presupposes by way of background social theory is the vague socialism of the New Left. It presupposes that there is a standard of free association of persons as affirmed in the anarchist interpretation of Marx, and claims to explain how that standard has not hitherto been attained in human society, and how it can be attained in the future through the liberation of women. Thus radical feminism is for the most part a form of socialist feminism, and in terms of a general conception of the socialist idea there cannot be any opposition between radical feminism and socialism.[46] However, there is an opposition between a radical feminism which affirms the primacy of the sexual war in the historical struggle for liberation and a Marxist socialism which gives primacy to the class struggle centred on the mode of production.

There have, nevertheless, been attempts among writers who call themselves Marxists to use the insights of radical feminism to supplement the deficiencies which they observe in traditional Marxist theory and practice on the woman question. The most notable of these is Juliet Mitchell. She argues that Marxist theory has a need for a specific view of women's oppression. The classic socialist feminists, such as Fourier, Marx, Engels and Bebel, treat the liberation of women as a normative ideal, an adjunct to socialist theory, but not structurally integrated with it.[47] They conceive women's oppression to be the product of the institutions of private property; hence it is for them sufficient to abolish these institutions to remove women's oppression. But the inadequacy of this view in practice has been established for Mitchell.

Thus she sets out to analyse woman's peculiar oppression in a way which goes beyond the simple economic theory of it. The aim of such an analysis, she says, is to understand why women have always been oppressed and how they are oppressed now. These questions she says are feminist questions, to which she seeks Marxist answers. Fundamental to woman's oppression is, of course, the family; but past socialist theory, according to Mitchell, has failed to differentiate woman's condition into its separate structures. These are: (1) production, (2) reproduction, (3) sexuality and (4) the socialization of children. On the first of these Mitchell criticizes what she calls the traditional socialist view that women are assigned less arduous tasks in the division of labour on account of their physical weakness. This to Mitchell is a major oversimplification; it is woman's lesser capacity for violence as well as for work which has brought about her subordination in the division of labour. Social coercion by men contributed to the formation of the category of woman's work. She was assumed to be less good at hunting and suchlike tasks, and consequently relegated to domestic labour. But it was her social weakness not her physical weakness that led to this situation. By ignoring this dimension socialists optimistically assume that with the development of machinery woman's weakness will cease to be a factor limiting her participation as an equal in the labour force.[48]

With regard to the second factor, Mitchell accepts that woman's role in reproduction has been the cause of her absence from the determining sphere of production, but denies that this factor is absolutely decisive. It is rather the basis for the idea of woman's role in the home, as distinguished from man's role in production. To overcome this factor it is not sufficient to say with the classic socialists – abolish the family. This is indeed necessary, but in order to pursue an effective policy on this issue, one must study the structures of the family, namely reproduction, sexuality, and socialization of children. With regard to reproduction, easy and effective contraception should make child-bearing totally voluntary, and hence completely change its significance for women. It becomes one option among others. The fact of overwhelming significance, she thinks, is that contraception dissoci-

131

ates sexual from reproductive experience, which, she believes, all contemporary ideology tries to make inseparable as the raison d'être of the family.

Thirdly, in respect of sexuality, the new sexual freedom of contemporary society has, because of the unequal power of men and women, led to women's further exploitation. But with equality sexual freedom would not be exploitative and would undermine the family. Lastly woman's biological destiny as mother was the basis for her cultural vocation as socializer of children. This allocation of roles is a purely cultural phenomenon. There is no reason why the biological and social mother should coincide.

These four structures must be transformed if the liberation of women is to be possible. Automation, Mitchell believes, will remove any residual physical inferiority of women as workers; contraception and sexual freedom will together undermine the family, while the socialization of children will cease to be done by families. Any emancipation, nevertheless, must concentrate on the economic element – the entry of women fully and equally into public industry. The error of the old socialists was to think that the other elements were reducible to the economic, and hence they limited themselves to the purely abstract slogan of abolishing the family without transforming its structures.

Mitchell's specific recommendations are the following: economically the most elementary demand is the right to equal work, but this must take the form also of the demand for an equal educational system. Easy and effective contraception and the abolition of the status of illegitimacy would contribute to the undermining of the family. The family as socializer of children must be abandoned. There is no reason why any particular form should prevail; experimentation should be encouraged. In general it is the family that is the source of the formation of the feminine character, and it is essential to destroy this institution.[49] However, Mitchell believes that it is already dissolving through the contradiction between its ideal of the unity of its members and the growing individualism of their aspirations.

One must ask in what way Mitchell's conception of the woman question goes beyond that of the classic socialist feminists, while remaining within Marxist orthodoxy. It is clear that she gives more attention to the different aspects of woman's situation in the family and as producer than did the earlier socialists who espoused the woman's cause. On the other hand the programme for liberation is in its main lines the same – a socialist society offering equal opportunities to women together with the abolition of the family. The novelty is supposed to lie in the denial that the abolition of private property and the entry of woman into public industry will be sufficient to ensure woman's liberation. The specific structure of the family must also be transformed. But this is only another way of saying that the family must be abolished and that specific policies are necessary to wean men and women from it. These will have to be some variation of the policies pursued in the Russian Revolution and written about in some detail by Alexandra Kollontai.

The fundamental issue from a Marxist point of view is how it could be possible for the family to continue in existence after the abolition of private property. Mitchell seems to be claiming that this is because the structures of the family are independent of the economic factor. Thus we need an analysis of the family and woman's position to add to the traditional Marxist conception. Such an additional analysis can be found in the insights of radical feminism. But if her view is that the structures of the family are really independent of the economic factor, then she is not adding something to Marxist theory, but rejecting its relevance in an important respect.

In her later work *Psychoanalysis and Feminism* Mitchell argues that the overthrow of the capitalist economy does not in itself mean a transformation of the patriarchal ideology, because the ideological sphere has a certain autonomy.[50] A cultural revolution is also necessary, and women can be the spearhead of the cultural revolution as the workers are of the socialist revolution. Some account is needed, then, of the ability of the patriarchal ideology to preserve itself under socialism, and Mitchell presses Freudian theory into this service. Although Mitchell criticizes in this work the interpretation of Freud by the radical Freudian Reich, she uses Freud in much the same way as do Reich and Marcuse. Freud, in her view, provides a true account of how the masculine and feminine personality structures are produced in a certain social context. Freud took this context to be a universal for human life. But if we abolish the family, we abolish the structures within which masculinity and femininity are formed. Thus Freud can give us an indispensable understanding of the psychological differentiation of human beings, and hence provide the basis for a successful attack on it. It is fundamentally the incest taboo, which is necessary for the maintenance of the family, that ensures the reproduction of gender differentiation. To abolish the family would be to remove the necessity for this taboo, and hence the reproduction of masculine and feminine personalities. These are not grounded in a biological differentiation, for the basic sexuality of the child is bisexual. Hence heterosexuality cannot be seen as natural, but is something learnt as a result of the family context.

Freudian theory explains the reproduction of the mental structures necessary to the perpetuation of the family once it is already in existence, but it does not explain the coming into being of the patriarchal family. At this point one might expect Mitchell, since she purports to be a Marxist, to appeal to a version of Engels's theory of the origin of the family. But since her aim is to show the 'relative' independence of the family from the economic sphere, she cannot afford to make such an appeal, and in fact seeks an explanation of the family in terms of the anthropological theory of Levi-Strauss as to the nature of kinship systems. Levi-Strauss, according to Mitchell, explains the basic family structure of father/mother/brother/sister in terms of the emergence of the incest taboo, the point of which is not the avoidance of the biological disadvantages of incest, but the creation through the exchange of women of an interdependence between a number of families, and hence the basis for a social interdependence larger than the family. The rules of marriage function as a means of exchange through which society is held together.

Once the family is in existence its psychodynamics is explained by Freud. We then need to know why the family is no longer necessary and can be dispensed with. This is because the original need for kinship structures to hold society together has disappeared, for society is held together under capitalism by economic ties. The family is redundant, and would have disappeared long ago but for the invention under capitalism of a new idea of it as a basic biological unit and a new function for it as the necessary means for the reproduction of the labour force. Were it not for the preservation of the family, the mass of industrialized mankind would have no need to exchange women, no need for the incest taboo, and could produce human social relations directly, without their differentiation into masculine and feminine forms.[51]

Given that one of Mitchell's main aims is to explain how the family is relatively independent of capitalism, the last argument, which purports to show that the family is really redundant but artificially preserved under capitalism, is hardly much to the point. If we concentrate on the combination of Levi-Strauss and Freud in Mitchell's work, can we say that these ideas adequately fit in with a Marxist theory? Levi-Strauss evidently cannot. It is quite incompatible with a Marxist materialist account of society. But if we ignore this, and assume that Freudian theory explains the perpetuation of patriarchal ideology, and hence the family, when the capitalist base has been removed, it must be said that this is compatible with Marx's thought only at the cost of making his theory utterly vague. Mitchell attempts to preserve the economic materialism of Marx's theory by talking only of the *relative* autonomy of the ideological sphere, so that it is possible to say that it is the economic factor which 'in the last resort' remains determining of the form of the other factors in society. But the appeals to 'relative independence' and 'in the last resort' do not specify the form of the connection between the relatively independent sphere and the economic base, and thus in principle allow for anything to be fitted into the general framework without possibility of refutation.[52]

Concluding Remarks

The basic idea of feminism in its various forms is, I have claimed, that woman is a free being, a person, whose value or worth consists in this nature; and in this respect her nature and worth is the same as that of man. The treatment of men and women in society must therefore be in fundamental respects the same. The difference between the forms of feminism, I have also claimed, derive ultimately from differences in the understanding of the way in which the freedom of one person, whether man or woman, is harmonized with the freedom of all; they depend on the acceptance of general ethical theories as to the nature of the individual's relations to others in a community.

In the relevant ethical theories, freedom is understood as the capacity of the individual to direct himself to ends of his own choosing, and worth or value attaches to individuals as such self-forming beings. The individualist theorist conceives this worth to lie in the individual as such, independently of his relations to others in a community. It is inherent in each individual as a separate entity, and a good social order is one which recognizes this worth by elaborating and enforcing firstly equal civil rights, which allow individuals an area of negative freedom in which to make decisions for their own lives, and secondly a set of political rights which enable individuals to protect and further those civil rights.

Within individualist theory itself a radical difficulty arises over the relation of one person's freedom to the freedom of others, a difficulty which can be understood in the form of a conflict between the claims of liberty and those of equality, or between the ideas of an older libertarian individualism and those of a more radical egalitarian individualism. On the one hand, the libertarians emphasize the importance of free markets as providing the opportunities for individuals to make decisions for their own lives by determining their relations to others on the basis of contracts rather than on the basis of tradition or of centralized decisions.

The unavoidable inequality of access to resources that results from the operation of individual enterprise in a market society, even if all start with an equal quantity of resources, is justified by libertarians as the necessary consequence of the basic right to freedom. The egalitarian individualist, on the other hand, holds that such an inequality of access to resources is a denial of the basic *equal* value of individuals as free beings which the libertarians themselves affirm. The problem of how to secure such an equality of resources produces further divisions of view, and involves egalitarian individualism in adopting socialist or collectivist principles. For one may aim to secure greater equality by redistributive taxation, or by cooperative production and hence collective appropriation and distribution of the product, and in either case the claim of the collective over the resources to be distributed is affirmed. Yet in all such egalitarian individualist views the primary value remains the individual as free being. The drive for equality involves the severe limitation of the freedom of individuals to make decisions for their own lives, even where those decisions do not make others individually worse off, but only lead to a breach of the egalitarian distributive pattern. On the one hand, the demand for substantive, as opposed to formal, equality leads to a restriction on individual freedom, which appears to contradict the basic value in terms of which equality is desired; on the other hand unrestricted formal freedom leads to substantive inequalities which seem unjustifiable in terms of the idea of the *equal* value of individuals as free beings.

A compromise between the extreme libertarian and egalitarian positions is to be found in the view that, while there is a basic right to equality of access to resources, inequalities are justified if they result in everyone being better off than they would have been in the initial egalitarian situation. This allows for a greater individual freedom than is permitted by extreme egalitarianism, while allowing it only to the extent that it serves the interests of everybody in terms of their access to resources (in the well-known theory of John Rawls, to the extent that it is to the long-term benefit of the least-advantaged group in society). Some such compromise may be in practical terms more sensible than either of the extremes, but it is still based on the individualist position which attributes worth to individuals as such, and cannot show that its interpretation of the values of freedom and equality contained in that position is rationally superior to that of either of the extremes.[1]

As I have indicated above the egalitarian individualist may in fact adopt collectivist principles for the production and appropriation of resources. This is indeed the case with the socialist William Thompson considered in Chapter 2. Such a combination of collectivism in production and individualism in respect of underlying value cannot be coherent. For collectivism in production presupposes that the collective and not the individual owns the individual's productive labour. The individual as a separate being cannot choose for himself how to express his labour powers in productive work, and this is contrary to the basic individualist principle.

The Marxist idea of socialism, therefore, in rejecting altogether the individualist understanding of freedom as being a form of alienation of the individual from his social essence, has more immediate coherence to it. The overcoming of alienation in Marx's view ensures that the individual in expressing his individual powers is at the same time and ipso facto expressing social powers which exist only partially in him and are completed in his relations to other individuals. There can be no conflict between the individual freedom and self-expression of one person and that of another or of the whole which unites them, since an individual is not a separate being, but the whole expressing itself in him.

The divisions of feminism correspond, then, with the above broad divisions between ethical theories that are grounded in the value of freedom. The classic individualist feminist of the eighteenth and nineteenth centuries is primarily concerned with securing equal formal civil and political rights for women, but not a substantive equality. Provided women had such rights, and thus had the opportunity to enter civil society rather than the state of marriage should they choose, and provided marriage itself involved an equality of rights, then in the view of these feminists the realization of women's free nature was adequately catered for, whether women continued to live a private life in the household or not. More radical contemporary feminists of the individualist persuasion retain the commitment to formal civil and political rights, but hold, firstly, that all women need to realize their freedom in activity outside the family, and secondly that inequalities of opportunities between men and women in civil society must be removed and a substantive equality between them must be aimed at.

The collectivist socialist feminist meanwhile, seeing women as, like men, not separate beings but in their individual labour essentially expressions of social labour, believes in the complete absorption of women into the public workforce on equal terms with men and limited by no private family or household tasks.

Radical feminism to the extent that it is an application of the Marxism of the New Left involves that movement's vagueness about the social or institutional form of the identity of individual and society. But to the extent that it adds to that Marxism the principle of androgyny, or the undifferentiated nature of men and women, with the corollary of the total abolition of all sexual role-differentiation, a new idea is involved which is evidently not derived from any more general ethical theory. At the same time it is not in itself necessarily tied to the socialism of the New Left and could in principle be combined with an individualism which rejects the family or one which rejects sexually differentiated roles within it, as well as outside it in civil and political society. It is at any rate clear that the principle of androgyny cannot stand on its own, but needs to be coupled with *some* ethical theory which explains how the freedoms of undifferentiated persons are to be harmonized.

With the above qualification in respect of radical feminism's principle of androgyny, it is clear that feminism arises within a broader ethical theory, and that the adequacy of a particular form of feminism as a body of thought must ultimately depend on the adequacy of the ethical theory in which it is grounded. That feminism arises at all in the context of these ethical theories is a consequence of the fundamental feminist affirmation of the nature of women as free and equal beings, and not dependent and inferior ones. Feminism claims for women the same ethical value that the general theory appears to attribute to human beings as such, but in fact limits to men. Furthermore, the reason that this feminist claim remains a controversial one and is not simply absorbed into the general theory is because it calls in question, at least indirectly, the organization, if not the continued existence, of what has been hitherto the fundamental social unit – the family.

139

The traditional pre-modern conception of women as by nature of inferior rationality, governed by emotion and instinct, was admirably suited to their restricted life within the family, since that life offered little opportunity for rational self-direction.[2] The early feminists' affirmation of a basically equal rational freedom immediately threatened the viability of the traditional family arrangements, although as noted above the early feminists in fact offered a compromise on this issue. To the extent that the problem of the family is not resolved practically by its disappearance or abolition or by the abandonment of sexually differentiated roles within it, feminism must remain a separate issue within ethical theory. For a society that attaches value to the family, and at the same time acknowledges woman's free and equal nature, raises the question of how the latter is compatible with woman's hitherto distinctive role in the former.

The problem with which feminism begins, then, is whether, and if so how, woman's nature and value as a free being is compatible with the nuclear family and with her traditional maternal role in it. In the classic individualist and socialist forms of feminism the sexually differentiated nature and corresponding role of women in society, if not in the private family, is not wholly rejected, but fitted into a general social scheme designed to provide for woman's realization of her basic worth as a human being as defined by the ethical theory.

Compared with these older traditions the contemporary feminism that affirms the principle of androgyny is committed to the much more radical solution of abolishing any special woman's role since it denies any special woman's nature. It may indeed look as though radical feminism could flourish to a considerable extent independently of any more general theory, that it constitutes on its own a more complete theory of woman and society than either of the older traditions, and hence that it can claim to be *the* feminist theory. This is misleading, however. The appearance of independence arises from the fact that, if the principle of androgyny is correct, women have to be seen as an exploited or oppressed class in a much more radical way than in the other two major forms of feminism. For it is natural enough, given the private family and given a belief in woman's special nature and its corresponding maternal expression, that women universally should have been left to private domestic functions of inferior worth in the eyes of a society whose public functions are exercised by men, even if this restriction is seen as an injustice and an oppression.[3] But, if there is no foundation whatsoever in woman's nature for this maternal role, then the restriction of women to domestic functions and the appropriate beliefs about sexually differentiated natures and roles must appear as a gigantic conspiracy on the part of men. The fact of women's oppression seems independent of anything else, and, since universal, prior to and more basic than any other form of injustice.[4] We thus appear to have the basis for the claim that feminism, as the study of the nature of this oppression and the possibility of its overthrow, must be a unique theory existing on its own. Yet a moment's thought makes it clear that any adequate theory of women's oppression and liberation as androgynous persons must presuppose ethical and political conceptions which explain the conditions for the realization of freedom for all androgynous persons.

The specific challenge that radical feminism presents is the denial of any biological basis for the differentiation of male and female characters actually found in society, and the claim that such differentiation is the product of social conditioning arising out of the assignment of the female to the basic role of mothering.[5] This issue is primarily one of biology, and a serious consideration of it would have to go deeply into the biological research on the matter, unless the research had already conclusively demonstrated the truth or falsity of the radical feminist claim. From my reading of some of the evidence produced on this matter, no such conclusive view has been established. It seems to be the case that, contrary to the radical feminist claim, the researchers *incline* to the position that there is a biological element in the differentiation of masculine and feminine behaviour traits, but the inclination is tentative or seriously qualified for one reason or another. One reason has been that a good part of the early evidence was based on experiments with animals, with the consequent doubt attached to any extrapolation of claims to human beings.[6] Nevertheless some of the more recent evidence from the study of human beings has led those conducting the research to make firm claims that 'there are in human beings some gender dimorphic behaviour dispositions based on ante-natal hormonal history';[7] that is to say that there are some sexually differentiated behaviour dispositions that are biologically determined. In this case the evidence appears to be qualified by the assertion that such differences do not uniquely determine gender identity, and this is understood by radical feminists to mean that gender identity is not biologically determined but is a social product.

There appears to be some confusion on the relation of gender identity to the question of sex-linked behaviour traits. By gender identity is meant the individual's own self-perception as male or female. There have been cases of genetic males, i.e. human beings whose hormonal structure is male, who have been successfully reared with female gender identities.[8] This shows that it is possible to bring up males to play feminine roles, that is to say to be caring maternal beings, and evidently the converse is true. But one cannot conclude from such evidence that there are no biologically determined sex-linked behaviour traits. One can conclude only that such traits are not so extremely differentiated that the male and the female in no way share in each other's characteristic traits. The fact that men are not incapable of 'mothering' does not mean that females are not more inclined than males by their hormonal structure to adopt 'caring' roles, and the same would be true of women in respect of the typical 'masculine' trait of 'competitive dominance assertion'.

If we reject androgyny and accept the sexually differentiated nature of men and women, do we have to return to the conception of their special roles, even if such a conception is combined with the claim that it is compatible with the equal basic value of men and women? Not necessarily. If women do have a different nature, if they are more caring and cooperative and less competitive than men, one cannot immediately conclude that therefore women ought to fulfil exclusively caring roles in private and public life, while men realize themselves in competitive activity. For from a socialist perspective competition is itself bad and co-operation should be the norm for society generally. Indeed one should perhaps conclude from this, as some have, that women are superior by nature to men – superior that is to say in their *particular* human nature, not in respect of their common value as human beings.[9] They are more fitted to occupy the leading roles in cooperative society. But this argument cannot be taken very far; for if men do not also possess the same cooperative nature, it becomes less clear that socialism is the appropriate form of social organization for human beings generally. A more plausible view would be that, while the cooperative spirit is the essential character of both men and women, women have been less corrupted by the competitive nature of individualist society through their participation in it to a lesser degree than men. But once the true nature of human beings was developed fully in an appropriate social form, and the spirit of cooperation was everywhere dominant, there would be no need to differentiate between masculine and feminine roles. However, this conclusion also ignores the possible different particular natures of men and women.

If, on the other hand, we are inclined to individualist values and their expression, to some degree, in an open and competitive society, then the supposedly greater competitiveness of men is likely to result in their dominance in open competition, even if opportunities for women are otherwise equal, and their natural abilities are otherwise the same. As men dominate a field of activity more, the less will women feel at home in it, and the more will the successful women have to become like men. One response to this might be to advocate the practice of reverse discrimination, which would involve the allocation of a proportionately equal number of jobs in a field to women, irrespective of the merit of the male candidates for those jobs. In this way women's particular nature and values would become more influential in public life. However, reverse discrimination is generally justified on the grounds that women do not enjoy equality of position in society, as opposed to a formal equality of rights, solely because of the effects of the discrimination and unequal opportunities they suffered in the past.[10] If, however, it were the case that, other things being equal, men would always tend to do better than women in open competition because of their greater competitive energy alone, reverse discrimination could not be a temporary measure, but would have to become a permanent feature of the social order. Such a policy would involve radical interference by a central authority with individuals' choices for their lives, which is hardly compatible with individualist values.

It is true that there is a form of egalitarian individualism which requires that individuals have equal access to the means to their ends, and this can be construed as requiring that they enjoy equal positions in society irrespective of their particular qualities or merit. But egalitarian individualism, as I have argued above, presupposes socialism in respect of the ownership and control of production, and is individualist in basic form only.

Whatever the general difficulties that may arise for the attempt to realize equal opportunities for men and women if their particular natures are different, it remains the case that the great majority of women are disadvantaged relative to men in terms of their opportunities to realize themselves in the public sphere simply because of their continuing responsibility in the family for the care of young children. This responsibility produces a substantial inequality of opportunity which could be removed only by the abolition of the family or by the equal allocation of the burdens of child-care within it.

To adopt the latter proposal would be to decide to overrule the possible relevance to family organization and values of the different particular natures of man and woman. However, if we consider the family in itself and ignore its influence on the careers of its members in society, we cannot say that the equal value of the man and the woman is necessarily incompatible with their fulfilling different roles. As we have seen in some earlier feminists, particularly in Fuller, the idea of a differentiated nature and role in the family is not thought by all feminists to be incompatible with the equally free nature of the couple. But such a view is possible only if we can see the man and the woman as equal members of the same community – namely the family – and their different roles as that through which their mutual dependence and value as members of the whole is expressed.

If such a traditional role-differentiation in the family is to be justified in a way which is to be compatible with an attachment to the basic principle of the equal value of men and women as free beings, then it will have to be demonstrated firstly that the family itself, or more specifically its nuclear form, is a necessary institution for the reproduction of the values of free individuality in successive generations, and secondly that the unequal opportunities for women that are a result of it can themselves be acceptable within the terms of the basic principle. To support the former claim one would have to show, firstly, that it is primarily the nuclear form of the family that is adapted, both in regard to the relation between the married pair and in regard to the education of the children, to the values involved in the understanding of human beings as free persons. The marriage relation is conceived as resting on the individual choice and love of the couple, and the treatment of the children is based on the belief in the importance of cultivating in them their autonomy and self-expression. Secondly, one would have to argue that there is no collective form of upbringing for children which could produce these values more or as effectively as the nuclear family.

With regard to the justification of women's unequal opportunities resulting from their special role in the nuclear family it would have to be shown in *general* that some degree of unequal opportunity is an inescapable consequence of the pursuit of the fundamental values of the system, and in *particular* that women have opportunities to realize themselves in the public world, and that their opportunities are as good as they could be within the constraints arising from the pursuit of the fundamental values in successive generations.

Notes

Introduction

1. J.R. Richards in a recent eminently rational work defines feminism as a belief in the *unjust* treatment of women by society. This is not one of her better ideas: feminist writers have no doubt been moved by a sense of injustice, but a sense of injustice depends on an idea of justice, and Richards's definition allows any idea of justice, however absurd, to be the basis for a feminist position, if it can apply to women and is not realized by society. Thus someone believing that justice requires that women be confined to the home, which contemporary society fails to do, would count as a feminist. See *The Sceptical Feminist* (Routledge & Kegan Paul, 1980), pp. 1–2.
2. See V. Solanis, S.C.U.M. (Society for Cutting up Men) Manifesto (Olympia Press, 1967).
3. An excellent critique of the irrationalism of some contemporary feminist positions is to be found in J.R. Richards, op.cit., ch.1.
4. Many contemporary feminists are, however, individualists, albeit of a radical kind. Their position will be considered at the end of the chapter on individualist feminist thought.

1. Individualist Feminism

1. Some reference to these can be found in S. Rowbotham, *Women, Resistance and Revolution* (Penguin Books, 1972), chs. 1 and 2; J. Mitchell, 'Women and Equality', in J. Mitchell and A. Oakley (eds.), *The Rights and Wrongs of Women* (Penguin Books, 1976) and L. Stone, *The Family, Sex and Marriage in England 1500–1800* (Weidenfeld and Nicolson, 1977), pp. 336–43.
2. J. Locke, *Two Treatises of Government* (Cambridge University Press, 1960), p.287.
3. ibid., pp. 368–9.
4. ibid., p. 309.
5. ibid., pp. 321–2.
6. ibid., p. 337.
7. ibid., p. 339.

8. L. Stone, op.cit., pp. 240–1.
9. L. Stone, op.cit., pp. 7–8. Stone's view of the development of the family from the seventeenth century is corroborated with different emphases in P. Ariès, *Centuries of Childhood* (Penguin Books, 1973; first published 1960), and E. Shorter, *The Making of the Modern Family* (Collins, 1976). Stone argues that the nineteenth-century Victorian family was a reversal to a more patriarchal mode, connected with the failure of eighteenth-century optimism consequent upon the French and Industrial Revolutions.
10. Stone, op.cit., pp. 223–4.
11. ibid., p. 328.
12. J.J. Rousseau, *The Social Contract* (Penguin Books, 1968), p. 50.
13. ibid., p. 53.
14. ibid., p. 77.
15. J.J. Rousseau, *Émile or Concerning Education. Oeuvres Complètes*, vol. 4 (Bibliothèque de la Pléiade, 1969), pp. 702–3.
16. ibid., pp. 767–8.
17. L. Stone, op.cit., pp. 343–60.
18. For instance by S. Okin, *Women in Political Thought*, Part III (Princeton University Press, 1979). Okin in her criticism fails, like many contemporary feminists, to differentiate types of family, and treats Rousseau as an advocate of the patriarchal family with absolute authority residing in the husband.
19. For a short biographical account of Wollstonecraft and other leading feminist writers see A.S. Rossi (ed.), *The Feminist Papers* (Columbia University Press, 1973). For a fuller account see C. Tomalin, *The Life and Death of M. Wollstonecraft* (Weidenfeld and Nicolson, 1974). On the radical Dissenters see I. Kramnick, 'Religion and Radicalism: English Political Theory in the Age of Revolution', *Political Theory*, November 1977.
20. M. Wollstonecraft, *A Vindication of the Rights of Woman* (Penguin Books, 1975), pp. 79–84.
21. ibid., p. 88.
22. ibid., pp. 119–21.
23. ibid., p. 85.
24. ibid. p. 103.
25. ibid. pp. 147–8.
26. ibid., p. 260.
27. ibid., ch. 9.
28. ibid., p. 313.
29. ibid., p. 263.
30. For a recent general account of these movements which, however,

puts the emphasis not on the ideals of the movement as such, but on their social context, see R.J. Evans, *The Feminists* (Croom Helm, 1977).

31. A useful selection is to be found in A.S. Rossi, op. cit.
32. A.S. Rossi, op.cit., pp. 416–17.
33. For an account of Fourier's ideas see below pp. 54–61.
34. See on this and on transcendentalism generally O.B. Frothingham, *Transcendentalism in New England* (G.P. Putnam's Sons, 1880), pp. 297–8.
35. O.B. Frothingham, op.cit., ch. 7 esp. pp. 175–6.
36. I. Kant, *Fundamental Principles of the Metaphysics of Ethics* (Longman, 1962), p. 46.
37. ibid., p. 55.
38. ibid., p. 56.
39. For a good introductory account of the thought of Kant and of the German Idealists see F.C. Copleston, *A History of Philosophy* (Image Books, 1963), Vol. 6., Part II and Vol. 7, Part I.
40. M. Fuller, *Woman in the Nineteenth Century* (Norton Library, 1971), p. 44.
41. ibid., p. 96.
42. ibid., pp. 115–16.
43. ibid., p. 175.
44. ibid., pp. 169–72.
45. See H.L.A. Hart, 'Between Utility and Rights' in A. Ryan (ed.), *The Idea of Freedom* (Oxford University Press, 1979).
46. J. Bentham, *Introduction to the Principles of Morals and Legislation* (Basil Blackwell, 1948), p. 125.
47. See on this D. Long, *Bentham on Liberty: Jeremy Bentham's Idea of Liberty in Relation to His Utilitarianism* (Toronto, 1977).
48. J.S. Mill, *On Liberty* (Everyman's Library, 1944), ch. 3.
49. J.S. Mill, *Utilitarianism* (Everyman's Library, 1944), p. 58.
50. A.S. Rossi (ed.), *J.S. Mill and Harriet Taylor: Essays on Sex Equality* (University of Chicago Press, 1970), pp. 20–1.
51. Available in Rossi, op.cit.
52. ibid., pp. 56–7.
53. ibid., p. 125.
54. ibid., pp. 146–7.
55. ibid., pp. 148–52.
56. ibid., pp. 173–5.
57. ibid., pp. 178–80.
58. ibid., ch. 3.
59. J. Annas, 'Mill and the Subjection of Women', *Philosophy* , 1977.

60. A.S. Rossi (ed.), op.cit., pp. 236–9.
61. R.J. Evans, op.cit., pp. 211–28.
62. A work in which this transformation is charted and expressed is L.T. Hobhouse's *Liberalism* (Oxford University Press, 1964; first published 1911). See also M. Freeden, *The New Liberalism* (Clarendon Press, 1978).
63. A notable recent example of this newer and radical individualism is to be found in J. Rawls, *A Theory of Justice* (Clarendon Press, 1972). This theory is the basis of the feminist position of *The Sceptical Feminist* by J.R. Richards, cited above. The espousal of an initial right to an equality of resources is qualified subsequently in so far as these theorists hold broadly that an unequal distribution which makes everyone better off than one would be in the egalitarian position is justified.
64. For the situation in Great Britain see E. Vallance, *Women in the House* (The Athlone Press, 1979).
65. B. Friedan, *The Feminine Mystique* (Penguin Books, 1965), pp. 270–1.
66. ibid., pp. 292–3.
67. ibid., ch. 14.

2 Socialist Feminism

1. It is the major socialist theorists of whom it can be said that they have a partiality for the women's cause. There are minor writers who are vigorous opponents, e.g. Belfort Bax, *The Fraud of Feminism* (Grant Richards, 1913). Also, although the main socialist movements have been nominally supporters of the cause, this does not mean that the rank and file male socialist has been an ardent advocate.
2. For a general account of the variety of socialist ideas see R.N. Berki, *Socialism* (J.M. Dent & Sons, 1975).
3. T. Hodgskin, *Labour Defended against the Claims of Capital* (London 1922; first published 1825).
4. S. Edwards (ed.), *P.J. Proudhon: Selected Writings* (London, 1970).
5. See R. Owen, *A New View of Society and Other Writings*, ed. G.D.H. Cole (Everyman's Library, 1927) in which he argues that men's character is wholly formed by the environment so that if we make men cooperate in production and in other forms of life instead of making them compete with each other we will transform them into morally better, because cooperative, beings, and at the same

time into more effective producers.

6. Thompson's general social theory is to be found in *An Inquiry into the Principles of the Distribution of Wealth most conducive to Human Happiness* (London, 1824 and New York, 1971).

7. James Mill, *Essay on Government* (Cambridge, 1937), p. 45. First published 1821.

8. W. Thompson, *An Appeal of one half of the Human Race, Women, against the Pretensions of the Other Half, Men, to retain them in political and thence in civil and domestic slavery* (London, 1825), p. x.

9. ibid., pp. 89–90.

10. ibid., p. 199.

11. ibid., p. 205.

12. J. Beecher and R. Bienvenu (eds.), *The Utopian Vision of Charles Fourier* (Jonathan Cape, 1975), pp. 216–20.

13. ibid., pp. 139–42.

14. ibid., pp. 332–80.

15. ibid., pp. 169–76.

16. D. McLellan (ed.), *Karl Marx: Early Writings* (Basic Blackwell, 1971), p. 93.

17. ibid., p. 107.

18. ibid., p. 108.

19. ibid., pp. 133–45.

20. L.S. Feuer (ed.), *Marx and Engels: Basic Writings on Politics and Philosophy* (Fontana, 1969), pp. 84–5.

21. D. McLellan (ed.), op.cit., p. 147.

22. F. Engels, *Origins of the Family, Private Property and the State* (Lawrence and Wishart, 1972), p. 71.

23. ibid., pp. 87–93.

24. ibid., pp. 94–110.

25. ibid., pp. 113–14.

26. ibid., pp. 117–21.

27. ibid., pp. 121–4.

28. ibid., pp. 125–9.

29. ibid., pp. 135–8.

30. ibid., pp. 138–45.

31. A. Bebel, *Woman under Socialism* (Schocken Books, 1971), pp. 1–6.

32. ibid., pp. 187–93.

33. ibid., pp. 278–9. The commentator's patience here breaks down. The utter foolishness of the idea that there can be a centrally organized system of labour based on the absolute liberty of the individual should not need experience but only simple thought to discern.

34. ibid., pp. 343–9.

35. For America see R. Hofstadter, *Social Darwinism in America* (New York, 1969).
36. C.P. Gilman, *Women and Economics* (Harper Torchbook, 1966), pp. 5–7.
37. ibid., pp. 37–9.
38. ibid., p. 49.
39. ibid., p. 107.
40. ibid., pp. 213–16.
41. For a recent biography of Kollontai see C. Porter, *Alexandra Kollontai* (Virago, 1980).
42. A. Holt, *Selected Writings of Alexandra Kollontai* (Allison and Busby, 1977), p. 58.
43. A. Kollontai, *Women Workers Struggle for Their Rights* (Falling Wall Press, 1973), p. 16.
44. A. Holt, op. cit., pp. 134–5.
45. ibid., pp. 142–9.
46. ibid., pp. 227–31; also pp. 276–92.
47. S. Rowbotham, op.cit., p. 153.
48. A. Holt, op.cit., pp. 237–49; also pp. 285–90.
49. On the position of women in the Soviet Union and other socialist states see S. Rowbotham, op.cit., chs. 6–8. For further reading see her bibliography.

3 Radical Feminism

1. S. de Beauvoir, *The Second Sex* (Penguin Books, 1972; first published in France, 1949 and translated into English, 1953), p. 28.
2. ibid., pp. 16–20.
3. ibid., p. 69.
4. ibid., pp. 69–83.
5. ibid., pp. 89–90.
6. ibid., p. 96.
7. ibid., p. 141.
8. ibid., pp. 168–9.
9. ibid., pp. 496–500.
10. ibid., pp. 733–41.
11. E. Figes, *Patriarchal Attitudes* (Panther Books, 1972), pp. 7–14.
12. For an account of the New Left which makes the connection between it and contemporary feminism see R.N. Berki, op.cit., ch. 9.
13. W. Reich, *The Sexual Revolution* (Peter Nevitt and Vision Press, 1951) p. xix.
14. ibid., pp. 73–9.

15. H. Marcuse, *Eros and Civilization* (Beacon Press, 1955), pp. 4–5.
16. ibid., pp. 40–1.
17. ibid., pp. 96–9.
18. ibid., pp. 151–4.
19. ibid., pp. 226–8.
20. H. Marcuse, *One Dimensional Man* (Routledge and Kegan Paul, 1964).
21. G. Greer, *The Female Eunuch* (Paladin, 1971), p.11.
22. ibid., pp. 18–20.
23. ibid., p. 14.
24. ibid., pp. 58–60.
25. ibid., pp. 219–38.
26. ibid., p. 140.
27. ibid., pp. 157–8.
28. ibid., pp. 326–31.
29. K. Millet, *Sexual Politics* (Virago, 1977).
30. ibid., pp. 25–6.
31. ibid., pp. 26–33.
32. ibid., pp. 35–6.
33. ibid., pp. 36–9.
34. ibid., p. 126.
35. S. Firestone, *The Dialectic of Sex* (The Women's Press, 1979).
36. ibid., pp. 16–17.
37. ibid., pp. 18–19.
38. ibid., p. 20.
39. ibid., pp. 61–3.
40. P. Ariès, *Centuries of Childhood*, referred to in ch. 1.
41. S. Firestone, op.cit., p. 102.
42. ibid., pp. 183–92.
43. ibid., ch. 10.
44. A. de Koedt, 'Lesbianism and Feminism' in A. de Koedt, E. Levine and A. Rapone (eds.), *Radical Feminism* (Quadrangle, 1973), p.246. See also in the same volume, Radicalesbians, 'The Woman Identified Woman'.
45. G. Rubin, 'The Traffic in Women: Notes on the "Political Economy" of Sex' in R.R. Reiter (ed.), *Toward an Anthropology of Women* (Monthly Review Press, 1975), p. 204.
46. The inspiration of the radical feminists discussed in the text is, as I have argued there, clearly the socialism of the New Left. But if one concentrates on the idea of the total abolition of all sex-role differentiation in society and on the creation of an androgynous world, there is no reason in principle why such ideas should not be combined

with an individualist social and political theory, although of course
in the radical form.
47. J. Mitchell, *Woman's Estate* (Penguin Books, 1971), p. 81.
48. ibid., p. 104.
49. ibid., pp. 149–51.
50. J. Mitchell, *Psychoanalysis and Feminism* (Penguin Books, 1974).
51. ibid., p. 380.
52. A similar attempt to use Freud and Levi-Strauss to supplement
Marx is to be found in the essay by G. Rubin, 'Traffic in Women',
cited above.

Concluding Remarks

1. J. Rawls in *A Theory of Justice* cited above does indeed attempt such
a rational justification. It has received great attention in recent years
for this reason, but few now consider the supposed justification at
all satisfactory. See on this issue my book, *A Critique of Freedom and
Equality* (Cambridge University Press, 1981).
2. For a rapid historical survey of such views of women see V.L. and
B. Bullough, *The Subordinate Sex* (University of Illinois Press,
1973). For the views of past philosophers see S. Okin, *Women in
Political Thought* cited above, and J.B. Elshtain, *Public Man,
Private Woman* (Princeton University Press, 1981).
3. It seems to be commonly accepted now that women universally
have primary responsibility for raising children, and that this in
itself goes a long way to explain their inferior opportunities in
society. See M. Rosaldo, 'Woman, Culture and Society: a Theoretical Overview' in M. Rosaldo and L. Lamphere (eds.), *Woman,
Culture and Society* (Stanford University Press, 1974). Also M.K.
Whyte, *The Status of Women in Pre-Industrial Societies* (Princeton
University Press, 1978).
4. Indeed from this perspective the oppression can seem so deep-
rooted in men's treatment of women that it can lead to the rejection
by women of any association with men at all, not simply as a
temporary measure with a view to the overthrow of male class rule,
but on a permanent basis. However, as de Koedt argues, in respect
of the manifestation of this attitude in feminist-inspired lesbianism
(see above p. 129) the attitude, quite apart from its impracticality, is
incoherent. It supposes that there is an opposition between men and
women inherent in their natures, whereas the idea of the crime of
men against women in the first place is based on the denial of any
difference in their natures.

5. For a study of this process from a radical feminist point of view see N. Chodorow, 'Mothering, Male Dominance and Capitalism' in Z. Eisenstein (ed.), *Capitalist Patriarchy and the Case for Socialist Feminism* (Monthly Review Press, 1979).

6. See the papers by Hamburg and Lunde, in E. Maccoby (ed.), *The Development of Sex Differences* (Tavistock Publications, 1967); and the papers by Green and Davidson in H. Katchadourian (ed.), *Human Sexuality* (University of California Press, 1979).

7. J. Money and A. Ehrhardt, *Man and Woman: Boy and Girl* (Johns Hopkins University Press, 1972), p. 117. See also E. Maccoby and C. Jacklin, *The Psychology of Sex Differences* (Stanford, 1974, ch. 10) and R. Stoller, *Sex and Gender* (The Hogarth Press, 1968), p. 74.

8. J. Money and A. Ehrhardt, op.cit., pp. 118–23, and pp. 151–62.

9. For instance Fourier, see above pp. 58–9, and Thompson, op.cit., pp. 128–9. Gilman also could be understood in a similar way, see above pp. 87–8.

10. On reverse discrimination in favour of women see J.R. Richards, op.cit., pp. 107–19.

Select Bibliography

The main works of feminist theory of the last 200 years are those discussed in the text, the publication details of which are to be found in the notes.

A convenient collection of excerpts from major writers with brief biographical details is to be found in:

A.S. Rossi (ed.), *The Feminist Papers* (Columbia University Press, 1973).

An extensive descriptive bibliography of feminist writing and writing on feminism is

S. Rowbotham, *Women's Liberation and Revolution* (Falling Wall Press, 1972)

a shorter version of which is to be found in

S. Rowbotham, *Woman, Resistance and Revolution* (Penguin Books, 1972).

There is little which, after the pattern of the present work, discusses feminist theory in relation to the tradition of Western political philosophy. However, the following two books do provide such a discussion, although with considerable attention to the justifications of the unequal treatment of women in the pre-modern period:

S. Okin, *Women in Political Thought* (Princeton University Press, 1979)

J.B. Elshtain, *Public Man, Private Woman: Women in Social and Political Thought* (Princeton University Press, 1981)

while a serious philosophical discussion of contemporary feminist thought is to be found in:

J.R. Richards, *The Sceptical Feminist* (Routledge and Kegan Paul, 1980).

Histories of feminism have little to say about the philosophical basis of the ideas of the movement. However, some recent general histories are:

R.J. Evans, *The Feminists* (Croom Helm, 1977)

E. Flexner, *Century of Struggle: the Woman's Rights Movement in the United States* (Harvard University Press, revised ed. 1973)

W.L. O'Neill, *Everyone Was Brave: the Rise and Fall of Feminism in America* (Chicago, 1969).

Select Bibliography

On the background of feminist theory in the political philosophy of the modern period see:

L.T. Hobhouse, *Liberalism* (Oxford University Press, 1964. First published 1911)

G. de Ruggiero, *The History of European Liberalism* (Oxford University Press, 1927)

R. N. Berki, *Socialism* (J.M. Dent, 1975)

L. Kolakowski, *Main Currents of Marxism* (Clarendon Press, 1978)

and for my own critique of these traditions see

J. Charvet, *A Critique of Freedom and Equality* (Cambridge University Press, 1981).

Index

androgyny, 4–5, 98, 108, 126, 129–30, 130 n. 46, 139–40
Annas, J., 38–40
anti-feminism, 1–2, 49
Ariès, P., 12 n. 9, 127
Atkinson, T.G., 129

Bauer, B., 62
Bax, B., 48 n. 1
Beauvoir, S. de, 1, 4, 98–108, 125
Bebel, A., 68, 78–83, 89, 91–2, 130
behaviour, sex-linked inherited characteristics, 109–10, 117, 121, 126, 128–30, 141–2
Bentham, J., 30–4, 50, 54
Berki, R.N., 49 n. 2, 110 n. 12
Bullough, V.L. and B., 140 n. 2
Burke, E., 15

Chodorow, N., 141 n. 5

discrimination, reverse, 143–4

Engels, F., 50, 68–78, 82–3, 89, 91–2, 103, 124–5, 130, 134
equality: meaning of, 1–5, 137; individualist thinkers on, 13, 18, 27, 34–6, 41; socialist thinkers on, 51–3, 75–7, 80–1, 88; radical feminist thinkers on, 99, 104, 108; see also freedom

family: nuclear, 11–12, 21, 118, 120, 139–40, 144–5; individualist thinkers on, 20–1, 28, 37, 45–8; socialist thinkers on, 48, 53–4, 57–8, 68–78, 80, 82–3, 88, 90–3, 96; radical feminist thinkers on, 102, 104, 106–7, 112–13, 114–16, 118, 122–6, 131–2
feminism: as movement, 1, 21, 42, 97, 116; radical, 4, 65, Ch. 3 passim, 130 n. 46, 139–41
Fichte, J.G., 23, 27
Figes, E., 98, 109–10, 117
Filmer, Sir R., 10
Firestone, S., 124–8
Fourier, C., 24, 49, 54–9, 68, 83, 89, 130, 142 n. 9
freedom: meaning of, 1–3, 136; relation to equality, 2–5, 7, 25, 43–4, 61–2, 136–7
Freud, S., 102, 111–14, 117–18, 127, 133–4
Friedan, B., 46–7, 109, 119
Fuller, M., 23–30, 36–7, 40, 144

157